NAMWAYUT

CHIEF ROBERT JOSEPH

KW<u>I</u>NKW<u>I</u>NXW<u>A</u>LIGEDZI WAKAS

NAM

WE ARE ALL ONE

WAYUT

A PATHWAY TO
RECONCILIATION

Cataloguing in publication information is
available from Library and Archives Canada.
ISBN 978-1-77458-005-9 (hardcover)
ISBN 978-1-77458-243-5 (ebook)
ISBN 978-1-77458-244-2 (audiobook)

Page Two
pagetwo.com

Edited by Amanda Lewis
Copyedited by Lisa Frenette
Proofread by Kaitlin Littlechild and Alison Strobel
Jacket and interior design by Peter Cocking
Front jacket photo by Hamid Attie
Case illustration by Andy Everson
Printed and bound in Canada by Friesens
Distributed in Canada by Raincoast Books
Distributed in the US and internationally by Macmillan

22 23 24 25 26   5 4 3 2 1

namwayut.com

THIS BOOK IS DEDICATED TO
the Survivors of Indian residential schools
with special remembrance for
those who never returned home.

These are the child heroes who exposed the
truth and the spectre of genocide.

Beyond a wholesome discipline, be gentle with yourself.
You are a child of the universe no less than
the trees and the stars; you have a right to be here.

And whether or not it is clear to you, no doubt
the universe is unfolding as it should.

"DESIDERATA," MAX EHRMANN, 1927

CONTENTS

———

INTRODUCTION

TREMBLED AT the sight of tens of thousands of people marshalling near the west side of the Georgia Viaduct for the Walk for Reconciliation in 2013. My knees buckled and my spirit soared in relief and intense happiness as the crowd grew to an estimated 70,000 people.

Earlier in the day I had my doubts. There was a torrential downpour and a chill in the fall air. I awoke at about 5:30 am and stepped outside to check the sky.

"Oh God, who will want to come to a walk in this kind of weather?" I whispered.

And yet, I was moved by the great importance of the moment. The potential impact for reconciliation was huge, if gauged by the size of the crowd. My doubt turned to euphoria as walkers continued to arrive under a sea of coloured umbrellas.

"We have come a long way," I thought as my mind flashed back to the day I left St Michael's Indian Residential School for the very last time. It was dark and

I had felt hopeless despair; that day, no one knew or cared much about little Indigenous children and the legacy of these schools. But the spectacle of wave after wave of umbrellas arriving from every direction pulled me back to the present. The crowd understood. There was a growing momentum for healing and reconciliation. The Truth and Reconciliation Commission of Canada had been travelling across the country holding gatherings to hear and record the experiences of former students of residential schools.

A few months before the Vancouver gathering, I was admitted to St Paul's Hospital for colon cancer surgery. While I was there, I was preoccupied with the pending TRC hearings. I wanted the hearings to be filled with people and to be front-page news; I didn't want them flying under the radar. I called my daughter to come and see me at my bedside in the hospital. Karen responded immediately, recognizing the urgency in my voice.

"Karen, I want you to do something for me," I said.

"What is it, father?" she asked.

I conveyed my concern that, with cancer, you never really know the final outcome.

"Although I feel good about my recovery, I want you to promise me something. Promise me that you will organize a Walk for Reconciliation no matter what."

There was a pause that seemed like forever.

"Consider it done," she said.

I was discharged a couple of days later but was rushed back in by ambulance with sepsis. In a few days, I overcame that and was discharged again.

I sat in my living room as Karen and her friend Chris Little, a brilliant accountant, put together an organization and budget for the walk. I didn't know it then, but that was the moment that our organization, Reconciliation Canada, was born.

At the four-kilometre Walk for Reconciliation, people laughed, danced, and cried. They hugged each other and shared stories. The sound of drums filled the air. Dancers performed along the way. We'd planned a four-kilometre walk because four was our sacred number, invoking the four directions. On that walk, we were coming together for humanity, for Indigenous Peoples, and for ourselves. Those who walked were giving credence to the collective will and desire for the cause of peace and reconciliation. The Walk for Reconciliation was designed to bring people together to call for a renewal of a broken relationship—or worse, a non-existent one.

The signs of hope and possibility were inescapable.

The walk opened with a profound ceremony to invoke the Nawalakw—the supernatural, the sacred. Two brilliant Kwakwaka'wakw Chiefs led and designed the spiritual invocation for the event: Chief Beau Dick, 'Walas G̱wa'yim, and Chief William Wasden, Wax̱awidi. The Chiefs led an ancient Kwakwaka'wakw ceremony seldom seen publicly and almost never used outside of their own territories, ceremonies, and Big Houses; in that way, we could share our spiritual oneness with the community. The Gilsg̱amlił, meaning the first or opening ceremony, mesmerized the huge audience.

Only a few moments before that, Chief Wax̱awidi broke the silence and anticipation by singing a chant as he spread eagle down to bless the happening.

I think one of the strongest visuals I hold in my mind and heart is the aerial view of the Georgia Viaduct, a route in and out of Vancouver to its east, seeing a sea of people: young and old; in wheelchairs and walking; Indigenous, Sikh, Chinese, and more holding every colour of umbrella. I remember the human sounds of feet on the pavement, and a lot of laughter. There were stories being told, people revealing their lives to each other, and the transformation of attitudes, minds, thoughts. I could feel it.

The opening flowed effortlessly from one space to the next. Singers and drummers in harmonious rhythm would sing a verse, and a curtain at the head of the throng would drop. Exposed behind the curtain were people in full regalia and wearing masks, representing every entity in the universe, including the undersea kingdom, animal world, sky world, and the celestial spirit world.

The moment was surreal, as if the contemporary and ancient had collided with each other, calling for a renewal of the relationship between Indigenous Peoples and newcomers.

The ancient Gilsgumlilth ceremony was intended to reflect the oneness and wholeness of Creation.

The Walk for Reconciliation was intended to invoke the oneness of humanity for Indigenous Peoples in Canada and all newcomers.

Other than the tears, everything was brilliant. And even the tears were brilliant. Tears are, in many ways, the key to moving forward. Tears mean that we have touched each other's hearts.

I was exhausted. I had spoken to everyone who would listen, both as I walked with my grandchildren Sadie and Thunder at the front of the line, and as I moved up onto the podium to share my thoughts with the gathering. By the end of the day, my whole body was cramping up and I had to be carried off the stage. But I knew now that people cared, otherwise why would 70,000 people show up in the worst of weather conditions?

As I lay down in bed that evening, I thought about all those people who showed up and took part. Each of them, all of them started by taking the first step to reconciliation. I imagined how many steps had been taken by all the people by the end of that procession.

All of those people had taken a first step.

That's how reconciliation begins.

RECONCILIATION IS a journey, always beginning with that first step and when that first step is completed, you take the next. The journey unfolds bit by bit, block by block. When that rhythm kicks in, you know that the process of reconciliation is underway, just like the unfolding flow of the Gilsgumlilth.

During the walk, what I realized is that while our work at Reconciliation Canada is the linchpin for moving forward, we need more voices. We need to talk more about our highest humanity, about our highest collective selves, making sure nobody gets left behind, and understanding that everybody matters. We have to start transforming relationships with ourselves and each other. Reconciliation belongs to all of us.

Reconciliation embodies the spirit of Namwayut, the idea that we are all one. One people, one community, one environment, one spirit.

At the walk, I began to see the metaphor in the language. When we speak the word "Namwayut," we are talking about the forests, the animals, those that fly and those that swim in the ocean, and the things we can't see or feel or touch in spirit. That which is everywhere and that which is nowhere.

Namwayut is one simple little word. It is an old-fashioned greeting. But this word also evokes the universe and the universal. This work evokes the music of the interconnected, the everything that we are together, all of the elements, all of the dimensions of what we know and do not know.

(1)

VISION

———

WAS UP before everyone else was awake. I didn't
want the others to see me in my hopelessly wretched
condition, slinking out of the bunk as quietly as I
could. I made my way through the engine room on
the boat, climbed a ladder to the galley, and stepped
onto the outside deck. Running to the stern, I flung
myself behind the huge seine drum.

I couldn't see much beyond my tears.

I heard myself saying, "God help me."

It wasn't intended to be a prayer. I had been angry
with the Creator for a while.

There were no other boats around. Over the gunnels,
I turned my head toward the shores on the far side
of the water. My eyes cleared up even as I slouched
behind the drum net.

As I gazed out at the body of water from Green-
sea Bay, I knew intuitively what was unfolding before

me was supernatural. There was an energy swirling through the water itself. Radiant coral, bright blue, colours that I had never seen before—all of the brilliant and dark shades of life together—limitless, unfolding beneath the waves.

I lifted my head, suddenly staring at the forest of Vancouver Island in utter awe. The forest was rich and dense, its green foliage shimmering with lightning bolts rippling through it from shadow to light. It had a lush green veneer with impenetrable density, revealing its grandeur and power. There was so much energy everywhere, cradled in each leaf.

Finally, I gazed into the heavens. The sky was filled with darkness and light. I saw the moon, the stars, and the sun. I had glimpses of the galaxy. For a brief moment, I observed Mother Earth. All of Creation was unfolding before my eyes.

I had no idea how long I must have been there, watching, feeling, in awe, in silence, but the vision ended as I heard a voice saying to me, "In spite of what you have done to yourself, you are a part of all of this and I love you."

———

SOMETIMES DIVINE intervention is the only force that can restore grace and sanity.

Before I got on that boat, I didn't want to live or die.

My drinking had really gone overboard, and my lifestyle was just risky, reckless. I would drink until I passed out and would black out for a day or two or three. Up until that day on the boat in 1975, I was haunted by my experiences of grave harm and loss during my almost eleven years at St Michael's Indian Residential School in Alert Bay. I carried unresolved trauma that I didn't understand.

It was overwhelming for my beautiful wife, Donna, and my precious children, Bob, Frank, Karen, Farrell, and Shelley, my baby. One day they packed up and left. I found myself all alone in our huge house in Campbell River. I responded in the only way I knew how, and even though I had a good job, I drank day after day. The days stretched into weeks—one of the longest binges of my life. I would go out as soon as the bars would open. Sometime in the late evening or early hours of the next morning, I would find myself back at home lying on the bed in the bedroom at the front of the house straining to hear my wife's footsteps returning her home. Trying to listen for the pitter-patter of my children in the hallway. There was only shattering silence. I would break down and sob myself to sleep.

One day, as I was walking in a stupor in downtown Campbell River, I ran into an old friend of mine, Sandy. I had been a crew member on his seine fishing boat for a couple of seasons.

"Wait up, Bob," he hollered at me. "I want to talk to you."

I was reluctant to face him, such was my sense of shame and embarrassment at what I had become, and I kept walking.

"I don't like what you're doing to yourself," Sandy said gently. "You should come fishing with me just to get you out of town. You know from before where my boat, the *Chief Y*, is moored. Go directly down there and sleep it off. We'll pull out early in the morning."

I don't know how or when I boarded Sandy's boat. The next morning, I opened my eyes and didn't know where I was. I remembered my meeting up with Sandy. The gravity of my predicament sank in. I was filled with self-loathing and self-pity. I was engulfed in a sense of darkness and I smelled the foul booze oozing through my pores. When you're an alcoholic, like I had become, you give up, you quit living. You don't want any relationships, not really. Because you can't stand yourself, you can't stand anybody else. You don't want to expose your vulnerabilities to others. So, you close in on yourself and you become isolated. You never trust yourself to get too close to other people.

You want to be invisible.

I was six years old when I got dropped off at St Michael's. Like many children too young to understand and cope with what they experience, I happened to be a victim of all forms of abuse that took place there.

Two decades after I had graduated from the school, the same memories would return, and my tendency was to drink. Everything on the surface was going well: the job, the house, the family. On the surface, I wasn't feeling too badly about myself. But like a soldier back from war, I didn't know how to handle those flashbacks.

It started with drinking on a weekend, then the weekend would turn into a Monday or a Tuesday. I did what I always did. I got dressed, went downtown, and drank again.

By the time Sandy took me aside and told me to get on that fishing boat, my life was meaningless.

I had been destined to be a broken human with no hope.

In that millisecond when I heard that voice telling me I was loved, I realized that I had given way to all of the hate and all of the cruelty and harm of residential schools. I had descended into so much darkness.

But I was loved.

I was *loved*.

Vision, or a message from the Creator, I don't know.

When I saw all of this, this brilliant universe, and was told that I was a part of it, then I knew that I did belong *somewhere*. Even for people like me, who had descended into so much darkness, I suddenly knew that we could rise above the darkness to bring light to ourselves and also to others. Deep in the recesses of my mind, I accepted that even though I was very broken, ravaged by racism and personal denigration, this vision gave me the courage and the momentum I needed. This vision became ingrained in my deep consciousness.

To acknowledge that I was *me*, that I was *loved*, that I *belonged there*, that I was *connected* to all of these things: the ocean, the forest, the heavens.

But old habits die hard sometimes. I crept back to my bunk and slept for a little while. Eventually that day, after we fished, we headed back to port. I borrowed a few dollars from each of our crew members with a clear intention to drink at one of the bars that evening.

I found a bar, sat down in the darkest corner that I could find and proceeded to drink.

Something was wrong. I wasn't feeling it. I couldn't reach a high to escape. Finally, closing time was fast arriving and I was still dead sober. I pushed myself away from the table and walked home to my empty house that I was trying to avoid because it was too painful to be there. I eventually fell asleep and it was the best sleep that I have ever had, then or now.

I have never ever taken a drink since then.

———

IT WOULD be another twenty years or so before I really thought about that vision and what it meant. By twenty years later, of course, I was involved with residential

school Survivors, healing projects, and supporting people in their court cases, one by one. And, in looking for
ways to resolve the issue of residential schools, I knew
that vision would carry me through all of the work.
There was so much despair among so many people, so
much hopelessness.

And this vision, it had come to be at the very heart
of my deep consciousness.

I knew that in spite of what I had done to myself, I
was a part of all of this and I was loved. If I remember
those words, then I have value and I have purpose. If I
remember that vision, I belong and I'm loved and am
connected to everybody and everything. It was a subconscious countering of the suffering that I had gone
through at St Michael's. All of the times that I was told
I was worthless, had no value, that I was too dumb,
and was too pagan. That I'd never amount to anything.

I was a child of an attempted genocide. Canada
was and is preoccupied only with my economic worth
and potential productivity, and, so I was asked, I was
forced, I was meant to comply with the killing of the
Indian within me. The killing of my soul, my culture,
and my language, and if not those essential parts of
my being, then the killing of my body. All that I was,
all that my family was, the fullness of our true human
worth, was sapped away. My spirit diminished, the
light dimmed from within me. If I would not accede
to being an economic cog in the wheel of a violent new

version of the world, I would perish and there would be no recourse for my family, and no newcomer would care. This genocidal path was set in motion from residential school to residential school, and then from child to parent and parent to child.

But it did not have to be that way. I did not have to succumb to the depths, to the worst of humanity. And if I did not, we did not. And if I did not even then, we do not even now.

As I slowly began to open my own eyes about our history and what was happening to other children across the country who went through those residential schools, I realized that we all needed to find some salvation from it. We needed to find a way to move from darkness to the light. The words I heard in that singular moment of clarity offered hope, not only for me, but for others.

In spite of what we have experienced, we are each a part of all of this and we are loved.

Most of us who left residential schools lost a big part of ourselves. Some of us felt as if we were nothing, seeing ourselves through the restrictive lenses of those who would wish us to be either supplicants or dead. And so when we left and we went out to the world, and tried to be like normal people, we could never be. We had not healed yet. We had not built ourselves up again. We had to get to a point where this transformation could really take place.

You see, we all discover ourselves in moments where we can find our own voice to elevate the dimension of who we are, from brokenness to healing.

What changed for me in that moment on the boat, and it was immediate, was the idea that I wasn't worthless and that I belonged to the human race. Over time, in that sense of belonging, I knew I had responsibilities. As a member of the human race it was my responsibility to talk about my experience, to talk about equality, inclusion, and love versus hate. This understanding underpinned my thought process going forward, so that eventually I was ready for the work in which I found myself. These were actual tools that became embedded in my psyche, subconscious or not, that I would need to remember to share with others who had gone through what I had gone through but had not yet found any enlightenment around it.

The message is simple: Create beauty and power and resilience. Do for ourselves. Regain our dignity, self-respect, and pride.

———

IN MY WORK on reconciliation, I've learned there are two kinds of people. There are people who have suffered like I did, in the ways that I did. And then there are the rest: good, caring people who listen to these stories and want to make things better, make things right.

And so, in telling my own story, I expose my deepest vulnerabilities for a reason. I've been there in that darkness, and I was able to rise above it. And so can anyone else. No matter where Indigenous Peoples find our inspirations, either through our own visions, or through our grannies, or our Chiefs, or our experiences, we can find the resilience to overcome our own suffering.

And for the good people who want to make amends with Indigenous Peoples, or who just want to live reconciled lives, I hope that when they hear my story, they understand.

I know we share a common humanity. What I want to do is to call people to think a little more deeply about this whole idea of human relationships, and how all of us, irrespective of the sides of the reconciliation equation we're on, can engage. You are each a part of the universe, and you may not understand *it*. You may not yet understand your purpose. But you're still part of this wonder. We all have parts to play, wherever we are in this jigsaw. And we're as big as we want to be.

The peak of human experience is allowing ourselves to know each other and ourselves. We are going to discover things about each other that will lend themselves to our shared journey, which will manifest in a higher level of humanity between all of us, in this country and abroad.

In spite of what we have experienced, you are each a part of all of this and you are loved.

(2)

CHILDREN AT THE CENTRE
OF THE UNIVERSE

T HERE WAS NOT a little child in G̲wa'yasda̲m's village
who did not feel loved.

G̲wa'yasda̲m's, on Gilford Island northeast of
Vancouver Island, is a storied village. Its inhabitants have been there a very long time, dating back to
their own Genesis. Our Elders boasted survival from a
warring raid by northern neighbours. The village site
is also a significant clamshell midden, a place where
humans came to gather. Carbon dating back more than
a thousand years proves continued occupation of the
site. The midden and village site are cradled by the
forest behind and the ocean in front. The traditional
home of the Kwikwasut'inuxw People, many groups
used the site as a winter village including the Gwa-
wa'enuxw, the Haxwa'mis, and the Dzawada'enuxw.

These groups clustered together sharing fishing grounds and traditions.

The Potlatch was our place and time for collective ceremony when our villages would come together, a Chief would share his bounty with others, and we would convene to make and mete out law on our fishing and hunting grounds, our land rights, kinship and family, and our inheritances. Even though the Potlatch had been banned by the federal government of Canada in 1884 as a part of the Indian Act, seeing it as a pagan relic that was nevertheless dangerous and wasteful and punishable by prison sentence, we found a way to practice it. The people—my people—were hunters and gatherers and the land was bountiful.

I loved our little house there overlooking the ocean. The front end of the house protruded over the beach; the back firmly attached to the midden site. When the tidewaters rose, the ocean flowed beneath our floor and the ebb and flow of the current and tiny waves could be heard. The ocean in front of us on any given day was a natural aquarium. Whales, orcas, sea lions, seals, mink, otters, and other creatures were on constant display as the ocean moved with the rising and falling of tides. Majestic eagles soared overhead while graceful ravens pranced the shoreline. Seagulls went about their awkward business scavenging for food.

A cluster of small rock islets lay in front of our home, accessible at low tide but we had to be diligent on the rising tide lest we became stuck and had to wait until low water or have someone come and get us if we couldn't swim ashore. My younger sister Na'di and I, along with other kids in the village, loved to test the fates.

It was at the water's edge that I never stopped looking outward to spot Sisiyuł. This magical undersea creature, it was said, had a humanoid face between two outstretched scaly tentacles, each with another head at its end. It swam in narrow channels, and if we happened to take a glance out to a nearby lagoon, it might be there. I would look out over the ocean with my sister, or my friend Basil, only to spot an orca or school of porpoise, but never the double-headed sea monster.

It was puzzling because he was everywhere else, it seemed. Sisiyuł was poised on the posts and beams of the Gukwdzi, the Big House, on totem poles, and on regalia like button blankets. He appeared in dances and songs. He crowded my little imagination.

From our parents, Elders, and Chiefs, we learned that the undersea creature had monstrous powers, both good and bad. His human face, the one in the middle, represents us—humanity. Sisiyuł's outstretched arms represent conscience, the idea of choice as a gift—as power. They equally represent the idea of balance and harmony. As humans, we can choose between love and hate. We can choose between right and wrong, light and darkness, good and evil. At the same time, we were told that if anyone gazed into his eyes, they would be turned to stone. Sisiyuł had shamanic powers, a warrior spirit, for good. Sisiyuł could heal us, protect us.

One day, Basil asked me a question.

"Chappie," he said, using my childhood nickname, "Do you remember the time when we saw Sisiyuł?"

I was a little slow to respond and that seemed to irritate my friend.

"Come on. Don't be so dumb. You must remember."

Basil said he, his grandfather James, and I were paddling around in a little dugout at the mouth of the lagoon next to the village. We were duck hunting and crabbing when we made the sighting. So I closed my eyes real tight and tried to remember, to no avail. If Basil was disappointed, I was even more so.

All the residents of Gwa'yasdam's knew each other. The only language heard in the village was Kwak'wala. People helped each other. If a family was sawing wood for the winter, passersby stopped to help. Hunters and fishers shared their bounty with other villagers.

The village and surrounding territory were like a garden of Eden, a paradise. Perhaps it felt like a paradise because, there, every child felt belonging and connection. There was not a little child in the village of Gwa'yasdam's who did not feel loved. We would always be greeted by our Elders with epithets that made us feel a part of a greater universe and a connection to a deeper meaning, such as Yo, 'Wadzid (Hello, monumental one), Gilakas'la, Długwe' (Greetings, my supernatural one), or G̱ilakas'la, Wołkine' (Greetings, my supernatural gift). Our names were often gifted to us in ceremonies, evolving as we grew up.

Children were the centre of the universe. It was for this reason that our law was created to place each child with the family member who would take care of them the best.

I was less than a year old when my father, Frank, passed away at the age of twenty-four, and the early waves of what the old people called Lax̱u'k'wala were sweeping through our communities. I knew that Lax̱u'k'wala meant coughing sickness, and, later on, I knew it as tuberculosis. I was too young to know anything firsthand about him, and, later in my life, I had to settle for tidbits of information. Coughing sickness was sweeping through our communities, something I heard often from his three sisters, Mary, Pearlie, and Susan, who told me that he was smart and handsome, ambitious and self-reliant. My father was also a musician, playing the banjo in the large village band in Kingcome Inlet. As one story goes, mechanically inclined as he was, my father was the first person in the village to install a high-speed engine in his boat.

He was also a spiritual man. In the days before his death, I was told, he reached out to his friend Sam Cedar. My father had a vision of the north end of the village right where the water flows. Behind that, he told Sam, there was a groundswell pool.

"Go and get some of that healing water from the K̲'uʼɫustola, the bubbling wellspring. Go and get that water and bring it to me," my father said.

Sam walked to the forest edge to try to find the pool. Nightfall loomed large. Sam came to a sudden stop as he tried to enter the forest. He was gripped in fear of what he might find there, so much so that it possessed him. Sam turned around and went to the regular well and retrieved some water there, thinking that it would quell my father's need. That he would never know the difference.

"No, that's not the water," my father said, pleading to his friend. "It's not the right pool."

Sadly, my father died that night, Sam by his side. He was buried at G̲wa'yasdam̲'s, where it is said that he had a spectacular Talking Stick tower over his gravesite. I found a small sense of faith in the spiritual yearning on my father's part, hearing the story. Nevertheless, I have long experienced a void in my wish to know my father and mother.

My birth mother had already had my older brother, and then me. Our sister Elaine was conceived but born shortly after our dad had passed away. It was too much responsibility for our mother to take care of three children without my father there to protect her, especially as she contracted the coughing sickness as well and was compelled to spend time in three different tuberculosis hospitals in Nanaimo, Bella Bella, and in Miller

Bay on the coast, separated from us by government mandate. Our family law demanded that we children needed more day-to-day care. I was given into the care of my maternal grandfather and his wife, my great-aunt Sally, my Ada. They already had a foster child, Na'di, and wanted to have more children. Our dad's mother took in my brother. Elaine was taken in by A̲nisbidu', another sibling of my grandmother.

We often went to my granny's house for weekend sleepovers as well, as all of the children in my family were drawn in close to listen to her stories. Her name was 'Nula'yi, and she was the eldest of a line of females in our family. Her traditional name was Kwi̲nxwa̲la'ogwa, Thunderbird lady. She had one single-wide bed up for grabs for sleepovers, and so my cousins and I would sleep crossways on the bed when there were too many of us, the last ones fighting for some blanket cover on the outside edges of the mattress. We younger children liked staying there, mingling with our older male cousins Steven, Jim, William, Tom, and Godfrey when they came to visit, to hear their stories as well.

Granny's house was a very small, dilapidated shack with no electricity and no running water, once only a lean-to, dangerous and useless, consisting of one room about twenty by thirty feet across. The walls were thin and there were cracks through which we could see daylight. In the winter months, strong winds with high gusts shook the whole village, tucked in tight in the valley, the wind going either upriver or down. Of course, the little house always creaked and groaned when stirred by the wind. The shack also had a special gin pole, about twelve feet long. When the wind picked up and the house was beginning to sway in the wind, the older boys would burst through the door to pick up the pole and move it to side of the house that needed to be held up. The pole would then stay there until the opposite wind arose. When the house was propped up, the shift and sway seemed minuscule, and there was no need to be afraid or concerned. Granny would make a fire in the potbelly wood stove. We little boys helped to pack water into Granny's house from the riverbank in tiny buckets, or a handful of wood when the fire was burning low.

At nightfall when it got dark, the adults would light up a gas lantern, pumping air into it periodically. If the lantern was lit and running out of air, it would begin to blink and stutter, becoming dangerous as the flames could easily blow outward and start a fire. At bedtime, the coal oil lamps would be turned on. I'm not sure why they would be left on, although at night I was happy to see the burning flames. I had the idea that the fire kept ghosts at bay, though I did not know where that idea came from.

When I stayed over at Granny's, my first chore after getting out of bed would be to bring out the chamber pots and empty them into the pit. Often our relative

Bob would stay with her. Granny was old, but Bob was older. He had snow-white hair and looked timeless, and his nickname was Ugwanu, white-haired Bob. As a matter of fact, I was his namesake. Elder Bob was iconic. He had a reputation for scaring kids and most little children were afraid of him, but he was really gentle. I liked him. When I emptied his chamber pot, he would always have a nickel he'd slip to me. Once, my brother got there before me and dumped the potty but didn't get a cent.

———

GRANNY SPEAKS to me even now in the yearning that I have to hear her voice and to remember her teachings. She wore soft shoes to walk the earth gently and to harvest the bounty of the land.

Granny would say to me often, "My grandson, you have to learn to love yourself. If you don't love yourself, you can't love others, and you have to learn to love others."

Granny considered the bounty of the land to be sacred, and that without it, we would be less. Her practices acknowledged the Creator that provided us with the land, and all who had come before us. There were prayers, ceremonies, and an acknowledging of our shared ancestral history. In the evening, we would gather up all the leftovers, open our little potbelly stove and pour the leftovers in there. We would tell the ancestors to be well. Her worldview was all encompassing. The sky world, animal world, mortal world, undersea world, spirit world were real for her. It was real for all of the others in the village too, and that meant that we needed to pay homage to all of those elements that made up our lives.

Love is the foundation of everything, Granny taught me. Love for the universe, for the world around us, for family, for self. Granny barely left our home territories. She stayed in our small areas, our small villages. People with one culture, one language, one spirit. And she was smart, because she made that choice to stay, to resist all of the forces that seemingly were against her, in order to devote her time completely to her family and children, and especially her grandchildren.

"Don't let the big noise bother you," she would say to me. "Be your authentic self, where and whenever you can. Hold on to those things that are of value to you. Truth, love, respect, humility—those are values that apply to any time, any culture."

Granny loved the Kingcome River, the estuary, the Gilford Island forests and beaches. She would bring us with her to harvest, gather food, and to demonstrate the sanctity of the wonder of nature in those places, reminding us to find peace and solace there.

Children in Gwa'yasdams learned who they were, where they belonged in their family history—their genealogy. We tend, as human beings, to give the best description to our realities. If we're all adopted into the same family, we will belong to one clan. None of the history ever changed. It was the same history that was taught down the generations since time began.

But what did change was who we were, and how each child in the village related to the world around us as we grew older. Throughout the course of their lifetimes, our people receive more than one name. The intention of how we name our people is more noble and powerful, in tune with the stage we are at, and how we are growing and becoming.

In an old culture, there are ceremonies that connect to the raising of children. It was understood that before ten moons, a child was still hovering between the spirit world and mortal life. Reaching this milestone, there was a formal ceremony to welcome each child into permanency in their human family and the human race. Adolescent girls, when they reached their first period, would also receive a special ceremony. Throughout the course of children's lifetimes, there were cultural markers for the acquisition of knowledge, of experience, to honour and witness and mentor and teach and *hold* children at each life phase.

Time was taken to make sure that children knew, understood, and felt the love at these ceremonies. Our Elders would always extend their hand to the child, and that was the intention when all of the people were assembled. As a witness, you are asked to walk with whomever it is that requires help and to always inspire them along the way.

Granny, my grandfather, and Ada, they taught me and cared for me, as did the other Elders called to my side as a child.

Granny was small in stature, but she was a giant in her heroic standards. And all of who Granny was: her kindness, her gentleness, her compassion, it still resonates in my soul. When I am still, I can hear her words whispering once in a while, reminding me that I am also a child of the universe, and that I am no less than stars.

———

EVERYONE ON Earth knows the word love. Everyone. I don't think there is a soul who hasn't thought about love. But for some reason, it's hard for many people to practise love. In losing that gift, it diminishes our own love for ourselves. It diminishes the possibility of loving people other than ourselves.

Over time, I have realized that if everybody started with love, knowing intrinsically that they were loved, the sanctity of life would rise as well. The creation of human life becomes more sacred, more spiritual. And when that happens, we human beings come deeper into our essence. Because then life is not only about ourselves, it's about everything.

And how infinitely powerful is that? And how infinitely big is that idea?

You and I are tiny in the grand scheme of things, but we are also a part of this universe. The loss of sanctity for people and for Earth is what has resulted in a desecration of our territories and lands. Our loss of moral compass as human beings is what is really creating hell on Earth, causing too much suffering for too many people.

Our human virtues are our values, our principles.

Living through our values means being together, being nimble, and being one with each other and one with all human beings, one with the animals, one with spirit. It is the interconnectedness that is missing when we don't aim to live as our highest selves, and we become singularly focused on just our own well-being, our own lives, our own businesses. We lose the prevailing need for care and compassion for each other. The rising anti-Asian sentiment, the need for Black Lives Matter, and the fact that Indigenous Peoples, of course, have been under the gun since the first European arrival on the shores of America—all of these issues can be connected back to a lack of compassion. We have to speak up and we have to make it right. And we need more voices that simply talk to and about our highest humanity, about our highest collective selves, making sure nobody gets left behind.

Granny's message to us was that the newcomers, who were destroying a lot of our ways, hurting our people, they didn't care about us. Even so, we must always remember that all of us still are one people. We have been here forever. They are here and they are not going away. We have to try and find a way to live together. Share the land, share the bounty. Talk to each other. Hear each other.

We all have stories to tell, Granny would say—every nation on Earth, every race on Earth. Everybody on Earth has a story to tell. It begins with the thrill and promise of a newborn baby's cry and ends with our last breath. We have one life, and living comes without dress rehearsals. Time builds upon itself, from Genesis to Genesis, from the beginning to the end, all matter has ever been interconnected. All humans have been one with each other. But the fact that our spiritual law has been avoided, this has brought forth much human error, anguish. In the miracle of life, we are not privy to a script or a completed master plan. And it is, then, in this spiritual void, when we stop telling our stories to each other, that the walls begin to creep up.

We can respect others, celebrate together all of our diversity and difference, and create the love and light that the world so very much needs.

Every child who experiences life should grow up to know that love, and what it means. Every child who experiences life should grow up to know what love names for each of us: security, safety, connection, and oneness.

Love is the foundation of who we are.

(3)

THE BOAT TO 'YALIS

"COME IN now, it's time to eat," my Ada hollered through the window.

We had been playing on the waterfront with other village kids, and both of us being very hungry, neither Na'di nor I did any protesting.

Dinner was unusually brief and quiet but I really didn't give it much thought.

"I want you both to be in bed early and to get a good night's rest, we are going to 'Yalis (Alert Bay) tomorrow morning," Ada said, clearing our plates. Ada had fully taken on the role of mothering me, as my birth mother had not returned from the tuberculosis hospital.

A few days earlier, when Na'di and I had been sent to bed, I heard Ada, 'Nula'yi, and Anisbidu' whispering to each other in our little kitchen corner. Ada was being admonished for drinking too much in her grief over the passing of Sibalxola, my grandfather. She

31

was told by her sisters that she would not be able to provide for us now.

While I hated going to bed early, I was thrilled about the trip to 'Yalis and thought little about what my Elders were saying. I tossed and turned and thought about the stores, cafés, and treats I would experience the next day. Just as I was finally dropping off to sleep, or so it seemed, Ada, my now-mother, was calling for us to get dressed and ready for breakfast. We packed our meagre belongings and trudged a short distance to the wharf. At the foot of the dock a little gas engine–driven boat was moored. Ada, Na'di, and I clambered aboard and settled in on the open stern.

It was a calm, sunny day with a slight breeze blowing. Luckily, Ada brought two blankets for us to share. As we moved farther out to the open sound, there was a steady, gentle roll of waves, and we giggled. Our view from the open stern was thrilling. First a pod of dolphins flanked us, as if an escort, for quite a distance. Then a pod of orcas saluted us as they passed us by, breaching spectacularly. If that were not enough, the sky world displayed its magnificence, as ducks and all manner of fowl serenaded us.

As we sailed past the southerly point of Cormorant Island, I spotted the Indian graveyard. There were so many totem poles towering, standing like eternal sentinels. The 'Namgis People had used Cormorant Island as a place to bring their people who had passed on. It was known as a place of eternal rest before the Europeans arrived. Missionaries forced the 'Namgis to give up their traditional practice of lashing the dead, carefully wrapped and sometimes boxed, to the branches of large trees in that place. A Christian graveyard was demanded by the Europeans, but the Kwakwaka'wakw placed memorial poles alongside the gravesites to honour their ancestors.

A year earlier a young boy in our own community had died at birth. The parents, wanting to follow the old ways, wrapped him up and placed him in a heavy canvas atop a tall tree. I remember seeing him swaying in the breeze, serene, gentle, and sombre. The authorities arrived a day or so later and ordered the baby taken down and buried.

I was born on September 15, 1939, in St George's Hospital, right next to the 'Namgis cemetery. In all of the trips we took over to Alert Bay almost weekly when I was a child, I don't know how I missed spotting St Michael's Indian Residential School on the north end of the island, but I did.

'Yalis, the Kwak'wala name for the place, means "sitting on the beach with legs spread apart," in reference to the way in which the shoreline at the village is shaped. We finally arrived at the dock, which clearly marked the divide between the Indian population and the white population on Cormorant Island, in the middle of those legs. Our lodging for the night with relatives was just at the head of the wharf. We dropped off our belongings and visited for a short while. The exchange of pleasantries seemed to go on forever.

The island was changing quickly. A hundred years before I was born, there were a dozen large communal houses at 'Yalis, and many had added one or more totem poles to the front of their houses like eagles, Thunderbirds, Huxwhukw birds, and a raven whose beak opened and closed as guests arrived for a Potlatch, along with human welcome figures to signal the ceremonies being held inside. Fifty years before my birth, there were only forty white settlers in the area; by 1900, there were 650; and by the time I arrived for school there were hundreds and hundreds more white people on the tiny island.

Now, both newcomers and the 'Namgis Peoples were flooding into Alert Bay to work the saltery and new salmon canneries, and it was filled with shops and excitement. I was restless and impatient. "When are we going shopping?" I whispered to my mother.

"We will go later," she kept saying.

At last we were out the door. The first stop was a little Chinese restaurant. My mother ordered hamburger steaks. The bottle of Coke and the straw topped it all off. The next stop was a little general store where my mother bought a pair of runners for me. I was so happy, I felt I could outrun the wind. The next items Ada picked out for me were a pair of blue jeans and a little white shirt. I had no idea what all her generosity was about. At the end of the day, we returned to our relatives' house for the night. "Coming to Alert Bay and receiving all of these goodies is reason enough to be anywhere," I thought to myself. We were ordered to bed early, my sister and I, and I didn't mind at all, even when I woke up a time or two to hear loud chatter and the singing of traditional songs. A rousing party was underway.

We were out the door early the next morning and started walking toward the uqsta lis, the north end of the island, in absolute silence. Our mother was walking in the middle and Na'di and I were catching up on either side of her.

"Where are we going?" I wondered to myself. "Why is no one saying anything?"

The silence continued, broken only by the sound of our footsteps over gravel. The streets were empty. We passed two older men sawing firewood on the beach. The only other signs of life came from columns of smoke rising from a few chimney tops. Still the silence prevailed. Suddenly, two adults came out of nowhere and grabbed Na'di. There was tussling and screaming, crying and shouting. It was total pandemonium. My mother, sister, and I tried to hold on to each other to no avail.

As quickly as the chaos erupted, it ended. I later realized that it was Na'di's birth father who had grabbed her. Ada was afraid of the authorities and so was Na'di's father, and yet neither of them knew what the better path was. Despite her father's efforts, Na'di ended up at another tuberculosis hospital before eventually being remanded to join me at the residential school.

My Ada and I hugged and sobbed for what seemed like eternity. We finally got ourselves together and started walking again. The silence seemed even deeper and more ominous, as I am sure Ada was doubting herself, what she knew, and what she should do. I heard the eagles overhead, crying.

As I watched the bird kingdom in motion above me, I caught a glimpse of the multistorey red-brick building ahead. I had never seen a building like that before. A knot built up in my tummy. I had a sense that this place was our final destination. The school property was completely fenced off. Two towering totem poles stood sentinel at the entrance. Each pole had giant Thunderbirds perched with outspread wings atop monstrous-looking grizzly bears. Each bear embraced a child. All figures had piercing eyes that were discouraging rather than welcoming. Both mythological entities represented supernatural power and strength, but none of that mattered that day. We reached the front of the building and climbed a steep set of stairs to the first-storey entrance to the school.

The front door of the building swung open and a strange-looking man invited us in. I had never been up close to a white man before. He spoke to my mother in a language that neither of us understood. My mother could only stare at him hopelessly. My fear was coming back.

"What are we doing here?" I thought.

From where we were standing, three long hallways stretched out to the left and right of us and straight ahead. All three directions had significant implications. Without a word, my Ada handed me over to the stranger. My mother turned around and walked away without any explanation.

Absolute sadness draped her appearance. She never looked back. She never said goodbye. I wanted to yell for her to take me with her.

She never said, "I'll come visit often."

She never said, "I love you." I knew that she did, but her grief overwhelmed her.

I was horrified and felt completely abandoned. Confusion and bewilderment added to my deep sadness. It had been quite a day already for a young boy with little understanding. First there was that long walk without explanation or understanding followed by the aggressive intervention and loss of a sister. Being dropped off with a total stranger in a hitherto unseen environment capped the evolving calamities in the worst day of a five-year-old. Little did I know that it would only be the beginning.

THE STRANGER took my hand and walked us through the corridor leading to the left wing of the building. The echo of our footsteps bounced off the empty chamber walls and collided and clashed with prevailing silence. The surroundings did not help. It was all so strange, and what was that awful smell permeating the entire place? I'd later discover it was disinfectant, but at that moment, I was acknowledging that I did not like this place and I was very scared, but there was nothing I could do. We exited a doorway at the end of the hallway, turned right, and descended two flights of stairs to the basement. We were finally in the bowels of St Michael's Indian Residential School. The stairway to the basement ended in a small open area. It was flanked with two doors on one side and a large double door on the other. I could do nothing but look up through the double doorway into a large play area, interrupted by steel posts holding up the ceiling above.

I spotted a child sitting in a chair having his hair sheared off while another boy waited.

My escort exchanged words with the barber and left. The barber talked to me in that strange language that I didn't understand and pointed for me to wait. I had lots of time to wait, and noticed two doors located at the back end of the playroom. The door nearest me was ajar and I could see little boys running around buck naked. They all had cropped-to-the-skull bowl haircuts. Finally, it was my turn in the makeshift barber chair. That day was the first time ever that anyone other than my own family touched me. I was uneasy and very uncomfortable. After my hair was shorn, I was ushered into the shower area, told to undress, and to fall in line where all the other little boys were standing. Everyone seemed embarrassed and all were trying to cover their private body parts with their arms and hands. It was humiliating, and very much in contrast to our ways back home. Nonetheless, the supervisor seemed pleased that he could chuckle at our expense.

Before taking our shower, the staff doused our heads in kerosene. The multiple showerheads were turned on and then from our queue we were herded into the communal showers. There were six showerheads in a tiny space and as we jostled for the shower, we acknowledged and bumped into each other, adding to our anxiety. A matron or nurse from the school infirmary was called in to do inspections. She poked and prodded in the most embarrassing of places much to our discomfort and extreme humiliation. The final insult for the day was the painting of our little bodies in a thick white solution. We were told to mill around for a few minutes while the white liquid dried. Then we were assigned our first residential school garb. We would never again see the clothes that we wore upon entering St Michael's. The jeans and runners that my mother had just purchased for me were taken away.

We were instructed to wait and play in the basement. A loud bell rang from outside the building and could be heard everywhere. For eleven years, I would hear that bell ring over and over again. Every bell was a call to rush to the playroom and to form a line in three age categories: senior, intermediate, and junior boys. Through the years there would be an extra line created for the littlest boys. When I arrived, I was the second youngest and the smallest boy at the school. Groups of older boys milled around staring curiously as we filed in.

I scanned the room and spotted my brother, Patrick, waving at me with a big smile on his face. "What a relief," I thought. "PAT!" I screamed, running toward him.

"'Walas ikin noka'yes kas yuwakus lox," I said. "I am so happy that you are here."

"Don't talk too loud in Kwak'wala or you will get into trouble and be punished," Pat whispered.

We found a small open space and sat down on the cold, concrete floor, leaning on a wall behind us.

"When did you leave Gwa'yasdam's and did Na'di come with you?" he asked.

When we were more or less caught up, he explained some of the routine and the rules.

"This room is the Am'lilas (playroom)," he explained. "You will hear a bell ringing loudly to announce supper time. It is your signal to find your way to this room to line up and then single file into the dining room. Listen to me, it is very important for you to be present and to fall in line when told or you will be punished. Always remember you are not allowed to speak Kwak'wala at any time here. You must respond immediately to all instructions," he emphasized.

The bell started ringing loudly at 5:00 pm just as Pat said it would. Those boys who were assigned to lines hustled quickly to attention for fear of reprisals if they were slow to respond. Pat raced for his line while we loitered, awaiting instructions. Soon we were in a line, too—for junior boys. Orders were shouted to move, single file, into the dining area. Both the single and double doors were open. The junior boys led the procession. I looked through the open doors of the smaller room and saw a long table draped in a spotless white cloth, filled with an array of dishes. The aroma wafting from the smaller dining room was tantalizing, enticing. I couldn't help it; I made a beeline toward the irresistible smell.

I pulled a chair out from the table and was preparing to sit when I heard Pat yell out, "STOP!"

He grabbed me by my shirt collar and escorted me back into the procession.

"This is the staff dining room and no students are allowed in there," he said. "Don't ever do that again or you will be in big trouble," he added.

I could hear chuckling from the ranks and felt humiliated. Pat pointed me to the double door entrance. The dining room was huge with low ceilings that gave it a cavernous atmosphere. Rows upon rows of long tables with wooden benches on either side of them stretched the distance to the far side. We filed in and stood beside the tables we were assigned to.

"Remain standing and be quiet!" the dining supervisor shouted.

I glanced at the other half of the dining hall, which was still completely empty. This added to the uneasy silence as we stood and waited. The double doors swung open and the girls started filing in. As we strained our heads to look, the dining room supervisor told us to mind our own business.

"You are not to look toward the girls' side. You are not allowed to wave to them. You must not communicate with them in any way," he emphasized.

The girls were as curious to see who was on our side of the dining room.

"You will find yourselves in deep trouble if you break the rules," the supervisor hollered. "Now all of you please clasp your hands together, close your eyes, and bow your heads so that we can say grace."

"For what we are about to receive, may the Lord make us truly grateful," everyone chanted. "Amen."

———

EVEN NOW, none of these are memories that we Survivors want to delve into deeply, for obvious reasons. But the truth of stories told by those who have experienced pain and who are grieving their own lives and the lives of their family members must be told. On my way to work this morning to sit down and write this book, I was walking through the community and an Elder came up from his house and hollered out to me. His wife has Alzheimer's and she speaks in Kwak'wala. Her memory is in her language. Recently I had been a part of a residential school Survivor healing ceremony at a big hall nearby, and we were able to share our experiences of our collective and individual grief and feel the healing that comes when we hold space for each other.

This Elder said to me, "With all of your life experience, you've learned a lot of things along the way, and our duty as Elders is to pass on what we have learned."

I agree. This is our duty.

My arrival at St Michael's was full of fear and confusion as I moved from a place of community and safety to one of anxiety. Not knowing what the rules were and why I was no longer surrounded by the love of my family, my life took on a different meaning—one of mere survival. We know that this brick schoolhouse, and others throughout the country, became houses of pain and grief for children. At St Michael's, the small open area at the foot of the basement stairway would become infamous for its gross violation of human rights against children. Abuse of a sexual, physical, and psychological nature, even torture, became prevalent. Children learned to live with broken limbs, children were placed in isolation in black closets often for days, and some children had needles pushed through their tongues when they spoke in their own language.

Yet sometimes, for some reason, when we go into our schools, in any places of learning, they are all sanitized. And by this I do not mean that our modern schools have been doused in disinfectant, taking on that horrible smell at St Michael's. I mean that, even today, there is no reflection of the reality of the dark and hurtful places in life in our schools' learning modules. We celebrate joy. We recognize history. We learn mathematics. But we do not actually learn about what is truly painful, and what it means to emerge from pain. Whether now, or in the past, our schools shy away from collective and individual grief, and what it means to emerge from grief. We still haven't really found a way to be comfortable with each other. Those who have and those who have not experienced pain do not know each other's stories.

We have the power to talk about grief and pain, and we owe this to residential school Survivors but also to all survivors of trauma. Until we start talking about it, nothing will change, nothing will improve. Dialogue in and through schools can absolutely create deeper meaning, a meaning that becomes respected and embraced by each other and for each other. Through talking about our pasts, we start to transform relationships.

We need each other. If we're going to transform and advance reconciliation, we have to bring everyone into the field. We all want to be healed, well, and balanced. Every incremental advancement is healing. One small step is a success. Survivors, and all people, need a welcoming, safe, and sacred space to tell our stories. We need to embed values for children from the earliest years through secondary school: respect for self, respect for others, balance and harmony, equality and diversity, do no harm.

Talking about our grief is what residential school Survivors are doing all across this land. In a generation or two, however, most of us who were there will not be here. But, in sharing our stories, our children and their children will hold a new perspective about who they are and where they belong. This is what is different; through dialogue and the recognition of our grief, all of us will be better for it—all Canadians.

When I look back on my experiences, and as difficult as they were, I am reminded of all that I went through. But more importantly, I can now carry a message to others who suffer similar experiences: there is hope beyond the conditions in which we find ourselves. For all of the harm and hurt and loss that I suffered, I use that as a reminder and a tool to hold myself up to my own chosen level of integrity. I believe that the more we share, the more this will be true for each of us. Knowing what we know about the pain of others means that we cannot, we *will not* inflict harm or hurt on anybody else. I believe this deeply.

My Ada had no choice but to leave me on the steps of St Michael's. It was not a choice to go or not go; it was a choice between being captured and forced and left quietly to my fate. My Ada had to comply with the mandate to send me to this school or face legal or criminal consequences, or she would have to hide me away like some parents tried to do, only to be found by the authorities. There was no escaping the laws of the Indian Act, one that had jailed and killed so many of us for decades, and which was increasing in its scope and mandate every year that passed: we had to assimilate. We had to become what we were not, or die trying. Both of us felt that grief and pain, as did every child and every parent.

But we would also learn strength and resilience, and we would learn to find ourselves and each other again.

We cannot go back. We must extract from all human knowledge a new collective worldview and tune into that together. You and I must be reconciled. Then it can cascade outward.

Each of us can become a wall against racism and hatred and abuse.

(4)

LEARN TO FORGET
AND TO REMEMBER

———————————

MY FIRST morning at St Michael's, I awoke with a jolt to the thunderous clanging of the school bell. Before I could clear my head, the supervisor stormed through the door in a fit of rage. He tore through the dorm flipping beds over and aggressively ripping bedding off others.

"Get up, you dirty little Indians!" he screamed.

I stood beside my bed stunned and confused as he ran between the rows of beds a second time.

"Get up and stand beside your beds, you savages," he roared.

His rage and rampage seemed to wear him down as he stooped over to catch his breath. The momentary pause was soothing but fleeting.

"When the bell rings, you useless kids have to jump out of bed immediately," he growled. "Now all of you filthy little bedwetters, raise your hands."

We waited curiously to see whose hands were raised. No one moved for what seemed to be forever.

"Damn it! Raise your hands, you stupid little idiots!"

Slowly, about six petrified children raised their hands.

"Have a good look at these stupid, lazy kids who should know better than to wet their beds," he said, to humiliate the raised hands. "They should be ashamed of themselves."

The boys who had wet their beds were ordered to bundle their soiled bedding together and stand in the middle of the dorm. The rest of us were instructed to form two lines by the entrance.

"Now listen carefully. When these stinking bedwetters walk between the lines, you smack the back of their heads or behinds."

As the boys jostled through the gauntlet with tears streaming down their little faces as they were hit and slapped, the shame and humiliation was inescapable. We filed out behind them as they made their way to the laundry room. The rest of us marched to the playroom where we washed up and dressed before being called to breakfast. The bell rang again, calling us to line up before filing into the dining room. I was so hungry and exhausted from all of the events that had evolved since my arrival yesterday. For a moment I felt so lonely and wanted to cry.

"Why did my mother leave me here?" I wondered to myself.

Finally, we were all in the dining room standing beside our tables. The girls on the other side were doing the same. Compared to the food I was used to eating at home, an array of wild meat and seafood, the residential school menu was bland and never enough. It didn't take me long to discover that some boys were served bigger portions than others. I learned quickly that when it came to food, there was a lot of horse trading going on. A tit for tat, a promise given, a promise received. You either learned to play or you were on the outside looking in to your disadvantage.

There were six children on each side of the tables. A senior student sat at the head of the table as Table Captain. The Table Captain's duty was to dish out the food evenly.

Breakfast was always a challenge. We had stale, putrid porridge every morning. Frequently, black worms danced and squirmed atop my bowl. Hunger will drive you to unimaginable heights, and I would simply push the worms to the side and eat from the middle. The skimmed milk was totally watered down and tasteless. The best thing about breakfast was the slice of bread spread with butter heavily laced with lard.

That morning, I looked around to see what the other children were doing about their breakfast. Everyone seemed to be eating naturally. I looked down at my porridge and watched as worms writhed through the mess. I took a spoonful and with teary eyes held back a heave.

Following breakfast, we single filed back into our lines in the playroom for the assignment of chores before classes. I wasn't assigned to do any chores because I was one of the youngest boys. My delight was short lived, however, when I was returned to the dorm for bed rest until lunch. There were about two dozen of us in our group. We were warned to stay in our beds, but we soon learned the routine of the supervisor and made the best of the day between his inspections. Sometimes the whole dorm would pillow fight. Other times we would simply stare out the windows. But the best was when we shared our stories of home and family.

At first, many of us didn't understand each other because there were so many different dialects in the school. As we grew to know each other we began to share the place names from which we came. They sounded magical and were pronounced so proudly. Every child had a faraway look as they recalled their homes. Greenville, Aiyansh, Kincolith, and Canyon City rolled smoothly off the tongues of the students from the Nass Valley. Still others came from Masset and Skidegate in Haida Gwaii. Farther south were Hartley

Bay, Klemtu, Bella Bella, Bella Coola, and Rivers Inlet. It didn't matter how many times we recited our places of origin, it kept us connected to our homelands. Maybe it was a way to bridge our constant loneliness.

When the weather was still good, we would be allowed to play outside. Soccer and Indian baseball were our primary sports. In Indian baseball, there were nine players to a team, and it was played much like ordinary baseball. One side would be at bat and the other on the field. There was a home plate and some kind of object like an egg carton acting as an outfield marker about sixty metres from home. Three misses at bat and you'd strike out, and a hit gave you the opportunity to tag the egg carton without being tagged in return. You could be chased and tagged down or you could be a target for a missile-like fastball.

It was not uncommon to recruit some of our home-language speakers to a team. They would then become the code talkers to determine plays, because there were speakers of so many languages among us— children who had been brought in from Bella Bella or even Tlingit territories, far to the North, depending on where there were places available and, sometimes, where they were caught by the Indian Agents who policed and oversaw each of our communities. Most times because of my age and size I would end up being a spectator. Nonetheless, being outside was my favourite place where we could escape the endless presence of the supervisors. We could also congregate with our own villagers and speak Kwak'wala without reprisal. An informal surveillance network grew so that the whereabouts of staff was always known.

———————

AT RESIDENTIAL schools, there was no possible way to *learn* anything. I did not experience learning; I experienced tension just waiting for the next slap across the back of the head. Waiting to stand in the corner. Waiting to be screamed at. My body was programmed to be ready to experience pain.

On that first morning, the teacher stood at the head of the room ordering us to line up.

"My name is Miss B, and I am your teacher," she said, her head turned away to the blackboard.

She then called our numbers one by one and escorted us to our desks. School officials would address us not by name, but by student number during the early years we spent at St Michael's. My number was seventy-seven. It was also the number with which my clothing was marked.

Her instruction was that we would file in and stand beside our desks every school day and that we stand at attention while we sang "God Save the King." The older students who had been at the school the preceding year knew the words and sang as best they could.

Those of us who were new could only watch and listen. We remained standing until the entire exercise was over. It was a while before I had any idea who this King was and why he needed saving.

For the balance of that day we were drilled about the rules. There will be no talking unless you are spoken to. You need to be absolutely still and quiet at all times. You must stay in your seats unless granted permission to leave. You cannot be late for any class. You must raise your hand to get permission to go to the bathroom. If you break any of these rules you will be punished. Many of the rules were no different from those followed by other children in other schools. But there was a difference in the punishment.

As the day wore on it became evident that Miss B was someone to be scared of. There were multiple strappings every day. Miss B would apply a ruler, blackboard pointer, or a leather strap to mete out her anger. Very quickly I didn't want to go to class anymore. I hated being punished for violation of the rules, but even more than that I was feeling sick watching other students being punished.

My growing fear caused me to be very careful about staying within the rules, and yet, being so young I was talkative and became distracted easily. It was in one of those moments that Miss B caught me from behind and cuffed my right ear. I almost blacked out and was overcome by the screeching in my ear. She then grabbed me by the same ear and led me to the corner of the classroom where I stood until the end of the day. The damage was permanent. From that day through adulthood, the infections started with the untreated rupture of my eardrum.

On numerous occasions students would raise their hand to seek permission to go to the washroom. Such requests were always denied, resulting in many wetting themselves. Other students were pulled around by the hair. No student escaped the abuse. When we asked for help, this added fuel to the fire as Miss B would go into a torrent of abusive and degrading words. The humiliation would be absolute and the shame complete.

It was a relief to hear the bell at 3:00 pm when we were dismissed from class. The next bell ring was at 4:00 pm and we fell into our lines and received a squirt or two of cod liver oil and a pilot biscuit. I hated cod liver oil but the biscuit lessened my hunger. The time between class dismissal and dinner was always welcome. It was usually a free and open period where all of us could play without being under the intense scrutiny of supervisors.

It was turning out to be a beautiful, warm evening. The ocean tide was up and calm. I noticed a barge on the water's edge loaded with wood that I later learned was intended for the school boiler and furnace.

"Hey, let's go down the beach and look at that barge," I said in invitation.

No sooner were we on the beach and trying to clamour onto the barge when we heard someone screaming at us.

"Get away from that barge!" a man shouted. "What the heck are you doing on the beach? You know that the waterfront is out of bounds. Follow me up to my office."

I turned around and recognized him. He was the man who had met me and my Ada when I was admitted into the school. Pat whispered to me that we were going to receive a strapping.

"When he starts hitting you, cry right away or he will keep strapping you," Pat added in a hush.

We filed into the entrance to the school and found ourselves right at the same spot that my mother turned me over to this man, who happened to be the principal at St Michael's. To one side was a small chapel and on the other side was his office. After verbalizing a severe reprimand that none of us could understand, he reached for a leather strap. Another one of my cousins was in front of our little procession so he got it first. The principal sternly ordered my cousin to hold out his hand with his arm extended. He raised the leather strap over his head and began the whipping.

After several strokes the principal stopped and asked my cousin, "Have you had enough?"

He was shaking in fear with tears streaming down his face. He couldn't understand English but sensed that there was a question asked. He took a guess and shook his head from side to side. The principal was enraged and screamed at my cousin to hold out his hands again, this time the palms down.

The strapping stopped, followed by, "Do you want some more?"

Terrorized and confounded, my cousin took another guess and nodded his head. It was almost too much to bear. It was my turn and I was crying before the strapping started. Pat was the last to receive a licking, but he never cried.

———

AT 7:00 pm, everyone had rushed to the basement playroom and fell into their respective lines. The senior boys' dormitory was located on the third floor; the middle school children on the second; the junior boys' sleeping quarters were on the first floor. We all single filed to our respective floors. We were led to our beds where pajamas were laid out for us. We looked at each other sheepishly as we undressed shyly. I had never been naked in front of strangers before. Twice in one day seemed almost too much to bear. We all stood by our bedsides until everyone was in their night clothing.

The supervisor started in. "Now everyone kneel down, clasp your hands, and bow your heads and say after me: 'Now I lay me down to sleep, I pray the Lord my soul to keep, If I should die...'"

The supervisor turned out the lights and locked the door behind him as he exited. The silence and the darkness provided a small measure of relief from a very difficult day.

My mind flashed back to the turn of events as they unfolded. It all started with that unbearable and unexplained silent walk to St Michael's Indian Residential School. Matters worsened with the sudden interruption and aggressive intervention with my sister Na'di being whisked away. Then the unthinkable happened: my mother turned me over to a total stranger and walked away without a word.

Everything had left me exhausted. Tears rolled down my face and I sobbed softly. I began to hear sniffling and crying throughout the dormitory. The floodgates opened and I wailed incessantly. I cried until there were no more tears.

But bedtime eventually became my favourite time, where I could imagine and remember what mattered to me.

I pulled my bed covers over my head and thought about Sibalxola, my grandfather, who had died a few months before I left the village. I called him Dada.

Dada had an engine-powered boat and took me everywhere with him. We hunted, we fished, we trolled, and we longlined for halibut. We went often to snag octopus and it was not unusual to have our tiny yard covered with octopus hanging out from the lines. We dug clams on nearby beaches and picked crab at low tide from the lagoon around the corner of the village. When the tides were at their lowest, we would spear for abalone and other underwater species, and grandfather would set up camp along the shorelines at night for small game like deer. Other times we would set traps in season for otter, mink, and the odd beaver. There were always geese and ducks to hunt. When my grandfather died a few months before I had been taken away from Gwa'yasdams's, it was painful to look out at the land and remember his kindness, the steadiness of his hand.

Dada was a big man with huge hands. I loved clasping my little hands in his whenever we went anywhere. I would be attracted by the orange-yellow hinge around his fists where the tobacco had stained them. I liked the smell of white puffs of smoke that he blew out. We went everywhere together as he was always busy providing for our little family. We would pull logs out of the brush for firewood. A favourite memory was drifting near a rock bluff where seals were known to inhabit. He would make noises like a seal and sure enough one would pop to the surface.

When I was five, Dada got sick and soon he was not getting up from his bed anymore. Relatives began to show up to visit him. One or two people would stay the night at his bedside. One morning following breakfast, as my sister Na'di and I were playing quietly in one corner of the house, we were startled by loud wailing.

It was my Ada and her two sisters weeping uncontrollably and shouting words to my Dada.

Eventually the turmoil subsided as others arrived to sit by Dada's bedside. A small group would come and leave and this would spur another round of wailing. It was scary and unsettling.

After a while my Ada turned to my sister to say, "Na'di, bring your brother out to play, but remember, no running around or talking loud."

We did as we were told and stayed in our little yard on the beachfront. Older men with tools and planks gathered in our yard. My sister Na'di and I watched from a distance as they began their activities. They took measurements and cut the planks. Finally, we heard the sound of hammering. We drew closer and saw the shape of a long box. Men huddled around their handiwork and talked among themselves. What came next was a total surprise. The men moved over to the tiny window next to the entranceway and began to take measurements. They removed the window panel and proceeded to cut a large hole where the window had been. The box was passed through the gaping space. An outburst of wailing erupted, followed by an eerie silence. After what seemed like forever, the box was passed back out in the same way.

We were taken to our Granny 'Nula'yi's house, Na'di and me. It was comforting to be with our other family members and away from all the sadness. Our uncles and aunts were caring and helpful as they explained what had happened.

"Dada has gone to a better place and is now with our wi ump (ancestors), and we will not see him again for a long time but one day we will all meet again."

I told my family about the people who had come and made a long box. I told them about the window being taken out and how the box was passed through that huge hole.

"When our loved ones pass away, 'Yax'id, they go to be with our ancestors. Dada was passed through the window and not the door in order for him to go on his final journey, and not keep coming back," I was told. "He would always come back out of concern for you. So, this is the way that we set him free."

Four days later, on a beautiful, sunny day at high tide, my Dada was placed in an open skiff and towed to a burial site south of the village.

The nights that I lay awake remembering bring to mind all the possibilities of intervention, including divine intervention. In times of great need, we never quit, we never surrender. Our Creator allows us to discover the human tools we need to survive what has befallen us out of no fault of our own. What I harnessed in those dark hours was a way to stay tethered to what made me safe: my memories of my Dada, Ada, 'Nula'yi, Na'di—all of my family.

At the school, it felt like being in a vacuum. Not being connected to others left me bereft in the silence of my own tears. It was an environment of hurt, suffering, denigration, and beatings. Everything about it was destroying who I was, taking me away from my authentic self and trying to make me into something else. And yet this was a destiny beyond my control.

Remembering the words of my family, holding on to those feelings of my culture, and preserving my connection to my birthright mattered. And I wanted to remember what it felt like to matter.

I wanted to be loved, I wanted to belong, and I wanted peace.

Just as in that moment in the dark on my first night at St Michael's, I still have many fears. Most of these fears are based on whether I have value, whether I have purpose, even now. And the only thing that keeps me moving toward the future is recognizing that I have the ability to stand my ground.

I am standing as still as a rock, giving weight to those things that matter.

Above: Kingcome Inlet Band with Frank Joseph, my father, at top right with banjo; my wife's father, Paddy Henry, on the drums; and Ms Arrowsmith, a missionary, playing the accordion in the middle.

Left: I am the second child from the left. This was taken near to the time I first arrived at St Michael's; we are all dressed in our coveralls.

Top: Alert Bay in the 1930s, similar to the view I had when I arrived for school the first time with Ada and Na'di. *Image E-04635 courtesy of the Royal BC Museum*

Bottom: Alert Bay docks in the early 1960s, around the same time I was working on the boats and ended up in the hospital. *Image I-28353 courtesy of the Royal BC Museum*

Above: Aerial view of St Michael's Indian Residential School, farm, and grounds (to the left), in Alert Bay in 1950 when I was still at school there. *Image E-04639 courtesy of the Royal BC Museum*

Right: A totem pole, one of two outside St Michael's Indian Residential School from the time I arrived there. *Image I-28360 courtesy of the Royal BC Museum*

Seniors
1955-56

Facing top: Me (on left), Stan Hunt, and girls from St Michael's Indian Residential School in Alert Bay.

Facing bottom: Class photo. I am first on the left, second row down (1955–56).

Above: My brother, Patrick Joseph; Ethel Wilson, our cousin; and me at the entry to St Michael's Indian Residential School.

Above: My brother, Patrick (bottom left), standing in front of the manual training shop at St Michael's Indian Residential School.

Facing top: My classmates in grade nine at a school concert; I am in the middle with the light jacket, smoking a cigarette.

Facing bottom: My adopted sister Na'di (Ruby) Dick Dawson Keetlah and Sally Walkus, my Ada.

Top: St Michael's Indian Residential School gymnasium Friday night dance; I am on the far left.

Bottom: Picture from my school days. L–R: Arthur Jackson; me at seventeen; George Wilson.

(5)

KNOWING TO WHOM
WE BELONG

I WAS HUNGRY all the time at St Michael's. There was never enough food and what we did have was awful.

I learned quickly how everyone dealt with their hunger. You bartered or you stole. It was a common practice. Slices of bread, biscuits, fruit, and other desirable items were all up for grabs.

One day a fellow student, Mark, had a family visit. I was sure that he would receive goodies from his relatives. I waited in the locker room area of the basement for him. Sure enough, he entered the basement with a brown bag.

"What did you get, pal?" I asked in my friendliest tone.

I was thinking he might offer to share and I wouldn't have to beg, but he slammed the locker door shut, turned around with a steely glare, and whisked by me without a word. My feelings were hurt, and I was angered. I walked outside to the playground and stuck to myself. I kept wondering what was inside that brown paper bag. Dinner came and passed and soon it would be bedtime. In the middle of my gloom and out of nowhere a plan popped into my head. I would wait until bedtime, when the lights were out and everyone was asleep, and then I would steal Mark's gifts. Just thinking about it meant that I felt a little better already.

Time passed slowly until bedtime, and finally we were all kneeling beside our beds, heads bowed, eyes closed. Eventually the supervisor turned out the lights and left.

I waited until the dorm was very still. There was a steady sound of snoring around the room. My heart was racing as I edged off my bed. I felt fear and excitement, tiptoeing down the stairs to the playroom, when I heard rustling sounds coming from the locker area. I peeked into the darkness and saw the shadowy form of someone digging into a locker.

I reacted instinctively by hollering, "Hey, hey, hey! What are you doing?"

The unidentified person dropped whatever he was holding, turned around, raced by me, and flew up the stairway. I was so frightened that I gave up on my plan to steal. I waited a few moments then clamoured up the stairway to my dorm, hungry as ever. Throughout the next day I kept looking over my shoulder and wondering who that person was, but more importantly, I was disappointed that my plan didn't work.

Stealing became an act of defiance and survival.

A stand-alone root house located behind the main building was an easy target to raid. It was always well stocked with potatoes, carrots, turnips, rhubarb, and apples, all from the school's own farm and orchard. It seemed strange that hunger was so common in a place that seemed to have so much, but the goods were sold to local and nearby neighbours in an effort to make the school pay for itself. Little of the produce made it to our tables.

My first taste of success at stealing happened when I joined a small group of boys in raiding the root house on a Saturday afternoon, when most of the student population was away on village leave. No one was expected back until at least 5:00 pm, and the staff on duty saw this as an opportunity for quiet time and let their guards down a little. We bided our time. At just the right moment we scrambled to the rear door entrance. Luck was on our side. The padlock was open. We jammed ourselves with mostly apples and potatoes then scrambled for the boiler room, a mere twenty metres or so across the road.

One of the boys who had obviously done this before instructed us to be quiet and told us to make our way behind two blazing boilers. There were crevices behind the two furnaces, and we placed our spuds into these spaces to roast. We stood around looking furtively in all directions while we waited. It didn't turn out too well, as the potatoes were covered in a thick layer of black soot, but that didn't stop us from eating the spuds. For some reason, we all looked up at the same time and burst out in uncontrollable laughter. Our faces were blackened and all we could see were the whites of each other's eyeballs. Someone in our small party suggested that Mr B, the engineer, might return at any moment. We all agreed and hightailed it out of there as he was mean.

———

ANOTHER ACT of defiance and survival was silence.

As we moved through the winter months, we remained indoors after dinner, clustered in an overcrowded playroom. Because of my age and size that first year, there was some concern for my safety if I was left to get in the way of the aggressive and boisterous activity of the older boys, and so I was assigned to the care of a seamstress who worked every evening in the sewing room one floor up from the basement.

Miss W would come and take me by the hand and lead me to the sewing room. On occasion she would pick me up. It was comforting to be held or cuddled by her. She was not mean like the other staff. Miss W was pretty. She had blonde hair, blue eyes, and ample breasts. She was caring and I felt safe with her.

The only time I felt uneasy while I was with her was when my peers taunted me, calling out, "Miss W's pet! Miss W's pet!" It was the evening when she led me to the sewing room for the last time. It had a table stretching the entire length of the room flanked by wall closets. Items of clothing, pajamas, sweaters, pants, and the like covered the table.

She locked the door behind her as we entered the room. She cleared a spot on the table, picked me up and sat me down in the cleared area. I had no idea what was going to happen next. She pushed me gently on my back and slipped my pants off. She began to fondle me, and I became very confused. I didn't say anything because I didn't know what to say. Although I experienced pleasant sensations, I instinctively knew that it was wrong for Miss W to do what she was doing. When she was finished with her fondling of me, she went on to conduct oral sex.

I felt guilt, shame, and remorse almost immediately. Why did it happen to me? What did I do wrong? Was it my fault? Miss W dressed me and told me to sit still until I had to return to the dorm at bedtime. She never spoke to me but acted as if nothing had happened.

I never talked about the incident to anyone. I never saw her again. She just disappeared.

Even as Miss W left, Mr C took up where she had left off. Mr C was a mean and frightening man whom I dared not disobey, and he was a supervisor in charge of the woodworking classes in an outbuilding in a shaded area near the playground. The younger children were issued denim coveralls that were supposed to be worn over pants, but as it got warmer in the spring, we didn't bother with the underlayers. Mr C would slip his hands into the openings in the coveralls and fondle my genitals for thirty to forty minutes at a time. I was frightened of the man, and my body experienced no pleasure, only the pain of knowing that the process would be repeated the next day.

Another staff person, Mr H, was very caring and attentive. We would go for walks in the woods nearby or we would walk to the waterline at the beach. We would throw pebbles to make ripples or wade into the ocean up to our kneecaps. He would tell us Bible stories and we learned to sing nursery rhymes. My favourite hymn was a song called "Heavenly Sunshine" that we sang all the time. I felt good and it seemed like a promise of better times. Mr H was popular among the older boys, too. He taught them calisthenics and boxing until he had a stroke and lost the use of one arm. But rumours ran rampant at the school. I was sad to hear Mr H was also said to be an abuser. It was hard to believe, but then it was also easy: we never knew what was going on behind closed doors.

While this was happening, Miss B continued her reign of terror in the classroom. I had learned all the words to "God Save the King," but there was a new girl in the class with a beautiful voice who elevated the sound and quality of the anthem.

"You have a wonderful voice," Miss B told Anne, the new girl, in a rare moment of acknowledgement.

Her compliment and show of kindness were short lived, however, because she caught Anne speaking to a classmate in Kwak'wala.

"How dare you speak that heathen language in this class when I have just told you that it is forbidden," she said.

Miss B instructed Anne to lift her dress to her knees and started whipping her calves with a long ruler with an iron strip on one side until the pain was too much to bear.

Later on that same week, I was very excited about learning to read a little book called *Dick and Jane*. It was so upbeat and colourful. I was attracted to the image of family and the fun they seemed to be having.

"Dick and Jane went up the hill to fetch a pail of water," I practised. I was so excited I decided to show it to my classmate Charles, who also spoke Kwak'wala, leaning over to his desk with the book open to show him the images.

"Du<u>x</u>w'wida's," I said in Kwak'wala. "Look at this."

Miss B caught me from behind and cuffed me on my right ear again. The pain was unbearable and I could not hear anything other than a roaring in my head for a moment or two. She then grabbed me by the scruff of my neck and led me to a corner to stand until lunch time, reminding everybody about the rules and warning everyone that if they were as dumb and stupid as I was, they would get the same.

She scolded me constantly, humiliated me every chance she could. She hurled insults at me. She strapped me often, sometimes with a blackboard pointer and other times a thick leather strap. I stood in a classroom corner for extended periods at a time. Miss B thoroughly enjoyed dispensing punishment.

———

I DIDN'T know where I belonged anymore or who mattered, and everything was confusing. All I knew was that no one was going to save me, and that the best I could do was remain quiet.

Even when I was quiet, things would unravel. Nothing seemed to be conducive to learning. A couple of years into my schooling, my teacher, Mr D, was a respected man with an army-type crew cut, which suited his strict authoritarian image. He was always stern and gruff, but he would catch me in a glance when my hair, having grown too long for his liking, would fall in front of my right eye and I would swivel my head backwards to clear my vision so that I could focus on the blackboard.

"Joseph! Get the hell up here," Mr D yelled as he motioned me to the front of the class.

He grabbed me by the shoulders and turned me around to face my fellow students. With scissors in hand, he grabbed me by my hair and cropped it to the scalp. The class roared in laughter at my humiliation, and with tears clouding my vision I caught sight of my cousin Pauline, bent over and roaring with laughter. I confronted her later and told her it was not funny at all, but the next day at school Mr D had Pauline in his sights. She had her V-neck cardigan sweater on backwards, which was the fashion at the time for many of the girls, and for this, Mr D screamed at Pauline and demanded to know why her sweater was on that way.

"Slut," he said. "Get up here and stand in front of the rest of your class. Adjust your sweater properly."

Pauline had to stand there while she squirmed, careful not to reveal her skin, twisting until her sweater was on appropriately.

Veiled racism was shrouded in these abusive and discriminating attitudes. Nothing really made sense. I thought Mr H was so kind. He wasn't my abuser, but he was an abuser. While Mr D was frightening and overtly racist, Miss W was kind and yet she made me feel shame. Miss B thought I was worthless and stupid. I was afraid for my life when Mr C called me into his workshop. And every day, I was too hungry and too tired, trying to speak and read a language not my own.

At St Michael's, I was told, "You're no good."

"You have no value."

"You're just a heathen."

After a while, a child just succumbs to the weight of oppression.

As a little kid, nobody's telling you to think for yourself, and when abuse starts at five years old, that kills the natural inquisitive nature that children should have. It's a done deal. You never think about what is right for you, what should not be done to you.

When you have no value to those around you, the response in your body is to be constantly at the ready for an eruption of violence. Violence can be a word, or a physical slap on the back of the head, or a kick in the back, or a sexual attack. When your every moment in those early years is brutally fearful, because of the cruelty of those who are supposed to care for you, your body adapts to the discipline, the monitoring, bracing for the next pain. With the hypervigilance that is ever present to prepare you for what will happen again, there's no peace—not ever. Unless you find a quiet little place under your covers or are lucky enough to sit on the corner of a soccer field and nobody's around to interrupt you—every moment becomes small.

Every child at St Michael's yearned for an open space around us where no one could intrude.

That first year at the school was the worst year in my life. And I think that, even if I had left after two years, all the damage had already been done.

All of us, all of those little kids, they must have felt like me.

I'VE THOUGHT about the story of my lived experiences of abuse a lot, actually, and the value of telling the truth. This story is a hard one, but it is one I must write.

All of a sudden, people have started to speak truth to power, and the act of defiance and survival is different from what it was in the past. But all of this matters because until the time when residential school Survivors started to tell their stories, we remained invisible. We remained unvalued. Learning about what we have survived has been the only thing that has really mattered to Canadians. Nothing else has moved people. And therefore, it is necessary to impose my truth upon the Canadian consciousness because the idea of truth in and of itself is a worthy pursuit. Since Indigenous Peoples in this country have shared this part of our truth, untold before now, we now have this opportunity to make some real change.

Telling these stories is important for Survivors, for people like me, so that we are seen, heard, acknowledged. And yet some days, I think that I should not reveal any of it. I am still ashamed of what I have experienced, even at the hands of others. I am still worried that I will be unvalued again, thought of as lesser than.

But the truth is more helpful. Telling the truth moves the needle that much more, inspires others that much more than staying silent.

Despite every single humiliating experience that I have had at the hands of those who worked at St

Michael's, and at the hands of those who commanded the school into existence, I know that sharing my life creates meaning. This is the most important facet of my journey. People who have lived a life like mine can rise above their pasts. There are too many people out there right now who have not come into this realization. Their children and their grandchildren also need to know that the past is something from which we can emerge, that we can transcend the lives that have been offered to us and know that we belong. That we are valued. That our cultures, our languages, the values that we share with each other and with the world around us are incredible gifts.

Every word, every discussion, every story we share facilitates change.

Unfortunately, we don't get to make the rules in the universe. We have to play through all of that lived experience. At the end of the day, the outcome is the outcome that was always intended by the universe. This absolute outcome is the only thing we cannot control.

Our words are important. Our ideas are important. Interaction and dialogue are really important. Our personal, individual, or collective intentions are important.

But in sharing our stories, in expressing and exchanging information with friends and others, that's when change manifests.

(6)

BOX OF TREASURES

THE WORLD came to a sudden stop one day. We froze in our tracks when we were told that our classmate Ray had died in an accident.

The day had started well, bathed by a warm sun and a gentle, rolling breeze erasing the last wisps of an overnight fog. A small group of us, all junior boys, were loitering on the north end of the soccer field close to the treeline. Most of the school population was downtown on village leave. Someone came running out on a narrow path from the wooded area, hollering.

"Ray fell from the swing. He is gone!"

All we could do was stand around wondering what had happened. I had seen that swing once before, but I was too scared to try it. The older boys wouldn't allow me to even think of trying that swing because it was risky, especially for a little boy. I tried to think about what might have happened. The tree that the swing was hooked up to leaned far out from the clay bluff. To slip from the swing was a terrifying possibility. Below that swing was the rocky beach—the beach to which Ray had fallen.

Eventually adults brought Ray up from the beach on a stretcher. As they drew nearer they settled him gently on the ground to inspect the damage to his body. I was close enough to see him, absolutely still with blood trickling from his nose and ears. They took him to the main building.

It was the last time that we saw him. The shock waves of the tragedy created an eerie shadow over everything. We children were left to loiter aimlessly on the playground. There was never any formal report, provision of counselling services, or even talk of what happened. I do not know if his family was told, except through our tiny voices on our travels home months later.

All was silence.

By this second year at St Michael's, I didn't know what to do with myself and my tiny body, so similar to Ray's. I had not yet learned to stand in line when we were called. The older boys complied, but I was distracted and would take longer to act in a way that was expected. One of our supervisors, Mr P, slapped me so hard from behind that I fell to the ground, landing on my left ear.

I lost consciousness and the world went black.

The older boys were looking into my eyes as I came to, searching to ascertain that I was alive and able to look back at them. They picked me up and took me to bed. That they were permitted to do so was a sign that something had gone very wrong.

My left eardrum was punctured, I learned many years later, and, as with the injury Miss B inflicted on my right ear the previous year with the back of her hand, I received no medical treatment. It became infected quickly and did not heal until I was an adult and was able to seek out specialist care for the bleeding and loss of hearing that followed me for many years.

As I recovered from my concussion, I thought of my Dada and his recent passing and I understood that in his passing, I would never see him again.

For Ray, it seemed like he just disappeared.

———

I FELT that I was disappearing myself.

I began to hear stories about Christmastime. I could sense the excitement about going home for Christmas for most of the boys in the school. I hadn't heard from Ada so I didn't know if she would come to get me for the holidays. I began to watch the southern point of Cormorant Island every chance I got. I would find a vantage point to watch for any boats coming from that direction. Soon, most or all of the students had departed by small vessels or one of the steamships that travelled the West Coast waters. I watched and waited right up until Christmas Eve. No one came. I received no messages. There was little to do. On Christmas morning I received a tiny black plastic gun. The only event was marching to the Anglican Church for Christmas service.

Before he left to be with our relatives, I had asked Pat about why I was not going home to see Ada, who had moved to a more remote inlet far from Alert Bay, over twenty nautical miles away. I always felt a little safer, less lonely talking to him.

"Ada's fine, brother, she misses you very much," he said in a hushed tone. "She just hasn't been able to come to Alert Bay to visit you since Dada passed away because she never ever has enough money and no boat," he added. From Kingcome Inlet, where she had moved, to Alert Bay by motorboat, it was a journey of eight hours, and one that Ada could not afford. "It's too far," Pat said quietly.

Tears rolled down my face as Pat tried to console me by telling me that he was sure I would be going home the next summer.

All alone when he left, I sank into a deep sadness, and cried and cried. I did not want to reach out to the handful of children also left at the school.

Sitting on the edge of the water waiting pointlessly for my Ada to pick me up, I looked up again at the eagles overhead. I saw a couple of ravens prancing gracefully. A little mink had scurried back and forth between the barge and the beach. Everything I saw reminded me of the traditional dancing that took place in our Potlatches, the cultural activities that I attended and even took part in. At St Michael's, I was learning quickly that the best thing we children could do for ourselves was hide: hide our bodies, our feelings, our tears. And especially hide our memories of who we were. Even though it was getting more difficult to remember my home as time passed, I found myself back in time letting the memories wash away the fear in my bones.

———

"GREETINGS, ALL my relatives, 'Namima," we would say to one another. "Namwayut. We are all one."

If a secret Potlatch took place at Gwa'yasdam's, boats would arrive from all the surrounding villages. People would arrive with their own bedding and mattresses, finding a billet until all the spaces were filled so that we would become one big family for three or four days. Those who were late would pitch lean-to tents on the stern of their boats. Meals during a Potlatch were all communal and held in a Gukwdzi.

The magic would begin immediately. One of the Big Houses at Gwa'yasdam's had a large door that opened at the top of a broad flight of steps, and we would enter through the mouth of a raven carved by kikua'enuxw, the artists who revealed our shared narratives through their blades. The same house was flanked by a totem pole, a small man riding a large whale that he had harnessed; between the whale's tail a raven, a flying Thunderbird beyond him.

Potlatches would go on day and night as the magic of the universe revealed itself to us through our traditions. A speaker, or hayak'ant'alał, acting as a master of ceremonies, would begin by inviting the k'wasanuma to honour what and who must be mourned. The imas, our founding ancestor spirit, would also be called upon to witness the transfer of privileges of those who had come before us to those who were with us now.

On the floor of the house, the dark and the bright melded into shadow with the brilliant reflections from the fire. A world of wonder emerged. The dancers, masters at drama, would share artifacts—symbols of our culture and our collective stories. Their dance masks had moving parts, and their feet would rise and fall in a rhythm of noise, a cacophony of singing and drumming and movement.

We little ones would simply fall asleep on the sitting platforms and then wake up to the continued unfolding of the P'asa. The Potlatch offered, and still offers, a monumental and supernatural blessing, and so many terms of endearment to small children. Every day, every hour, every chance somebody would tell you your worth and say you are special. You are precious. I would wake up, hear the singing near the fire, see the shadows, see everybody dancing, and feel safe because I would be sleeping at the feet of my Elders with all of the other children beside me.

Some of the dances were serious, and less peaceful. We children had to stay awake to learn about the wild woman of the woods, Dzunuk̲wa, who abducted little children and took them away and devoured them. You could smell her before you saw her, and you'd know her by the sound she made: "Huu huuuuu." Then there was the tale of the wild man of the woods, Bak̲'was, who would eat children at the water's edge. These stories taught children to be careful and not go too far over the river's edge or be attacked by a grizzly bear in the forest. There were even narratives to keep children safe from challenges close to home: A child who had to run away from an abusive father found himself in the care of a supernatural mouse, who brought him into the realm of the Atłak̲'ima, or forest spirits, who guided him to safety back home so that he would be welcomed into his village. Trepidation over these scary things at the fire's edge, as these stories were danced and explained to us by our Elders, meant that we were loved and we were safe.

————

IN THE POTLATCH, we are permitted to define the ways in which we see ourselves, in which we see each other, redefining our relationship as belonging together. We are allowed to move through wonder, fear, and grief, remembering and reliving. It has been that way since our Genesis, since the very first Potlatch.

But most of all we are allowed to see ourselves as part of a whole.

Dancers would re-enact the known and the unknown, the origins of our birth as human beings, and the beloved creatures of our forests, waters, and of the air. A speaker would identify our family, our extended family, and the fact that we each belonged to the same box of treasures. Chiefs had possession of these metaphorical boxes in which they collected everything of value: their family's songs and dances, their prerogatives. Our origin, our place in the universe, togetherness, belonging, all of who we were evolved throughout time, flowed from those boxes.

Masks adorned many of the dancers who moved about the Gukwdzi with grace as the drums beat from the back of the room, their arms raised, bodies moving in a singular motion, making each story alive for all of us.

Looking beyond the masks into the eyes of the dancers, we could see, could feel the universe.

Seeing through their eyes, we children reached another dimension, a deeper dimension that connected us all.

In that small glimpse of the universe was a deep yearning, a knowing, of who we were, of all that we were meant to be.

At the Potlatch, I learned to feel connected. I learned that I belonged to a community, to my family, and to something bigger than myself. I learned about the universe that magically unfolds from the box of treasures, to the dance itself, and ritual and transitional rites of passage.

———

IN RECONCILIATION, we must learn the same lesson.

When we are new to understanding, we are fearful. The shame and humiliation, the denigration of our Indigeneity and our Potlatch, our culture, and, frankly, everything about us, was a heavy burden. We have had to come face-to-face with some of our deepest fears. We have had to face up to feeling alone. And this can be just as true for some Canadians as it is for Indigenous Peoples; we all share the burden of trauma.

But when we recognize that we are all fearful, we can share this journey together. We can find our own deep wisdom. We can be hopeful.

We are all small, we are all mortal, and we are all caught up in the frenzy of feeling alone in the woods. But when we can think of ourselves as being part of this wonderful, magical universe, *we can't get much bigger*. We are bigger when we connect with the whole. We must acknowledge the universe, our own power, and our influence when we connect with the whole. When we acknowledge this, we know that we have the power to elicit the changes we seek.

In the simplest of terms, we have to exercise our connection, and we have to hold on to the immensity of the power that we have within that connection.

In so doing, reconciliation is an imperative for all of us.

The Potlatch can create a parallel universe in which our children can grow up to look through their own lens so that by the time they're adolescents, they will have a clearer idea about the universe—that everything we do is dependent on the well-being of others, of the environment. Ultimately, in this cultural practice, there is very little separation between ritual and ceremony, and very little separation between everything else in our world that we see and feel and touch, and even what is invisible to us.

But the same parallels can be created through reconciliation. Whether or not there is a fire roaring in the middle of the room on a dark, northern night, there can be mystery, there can be wonder, and there can be magic. We can live and breathe the cosmos every day; it can become real in our heart and our mind and our soul. We can meld with our collective wisdom and our deep yearning for a better Earth—a better way of a knowing who we are and what we were meant to be. This is what is truly magical.

As one, we can create what we desire between us.

(7)

WE ARE MORE THAN DRIFTWOOD

———————

O N THE residential school playground, I heard older boys chuckling and pointing to me as they ran around, turning their heads to look at me. I knew these boys—Dan, Thomas, and some others—because they all spoke the same language that I spoke, one of seven languages spoken at St Michael's and one of seven languages that we were not allowed to speak. Our forbidden words were like whispers most of the time. Except times like this, when our laugher and our joy couldn't be contained.

In Kwak'wala, Dan said to Thomas, "Hey, there goes your kid brother."

I couldn't understand why Dan would have said that to Thomas. He wasn't my brother. They laughed. Family remained with family, Pat had explained to me. I was beginning to understand why we spent time together at Ǥwa'yasdam's. Even our little houses were only a short distance from each other. My Ada had gotten together with Thomas's father, Chief Tom Dawson, after my Dada had passed away and after I'd gone to St Michael's.

Chief Tom Dawson had a big boat, and he and Ada could finally come pick me up for the summers. And so, I started my life with them together, again, in Gwa'yi, Kingcome village.

And everything changed.

Chief Tom Dawson, Ǥwa'yimdzi, was a fisherman. In late April or early May, we would fish eulachons the old, old way. Eulachons, ƚi'na, are smoked and dried, and vats of eulachons are fermented. Eulachon was once such a valuable commodity that trade routes in coastal British Columbia came to be known as grease trails. Its buttery flesh is so rich in oil that a dried fish will light and burn like a candle and can be eaten without anything added. We extracted that fish oil to create a vitamin-rich grease that could be used as medicine, as a salve, or for cooking—and that could be transported or stored without spoiling. I would run across the river to the eulachon pit to help. The smell of rendering grease from the eulachons was so pronounced that my fellow students refused to sit near me when I returned to class.

On the warmer summer days, he dried his boat on the beach and copper-painted the bottom, mending holes in his net and making sure everything was ready. I would tag along with him, going up the river to check on the nets that were strung out for salmon. There were no motors. He would pole us all the way up the river, and it would take half a day just to get there. We'd be looking at the gillnets, taking care to honour their one-way spawning migrations. We used modern tools, but in earlier generations, at the end of each net, a ring of willow was woven in to allow some salmon to escape and return to their home rivers once again so they could come back next year. And then, toward the evening, we would drift down the river and watch for deer or black bear. Chief Tom Dawson would be hunting as we came down, planning ahead, using every moment wisely. Steady.

In the summer, earlier practices saw the Elders cultivate the stinging nettles that would grow up around the village. As the summer ended, they would cut down the nettles to dry, so that they would become fibrous and strong in the last heat of the year. The fibres would then be spun carefully to make twine for the eulachon fishing nets.

In November, as I remember from my early childhood, we'd go up the river again to a permanent smokehouse. The whole family would go, maybe about fifteen to twenty of us, and for two weeks at a time. My chore was to pack water from the river to the shack, and to make kindling. The fire had to be stoked all the time as it was cold up there in November. The adults would harvest the fish and cut them up and hang them up in the same smokehouse in which we were living. Fish were hanging everywhere above us. After two or three more days in the smoke, we'd plan for home and they would take all of the salmon down. At night, all the ladies would sit around the fire taking out the bones from the dried slabs of fish. And, at that time, as the work grew repetitive, someone would be telling a story. At the end of chum harvest and dry processing, we'd drift downriver with canoes loaded to the brim with bundles of dry, smoked salmon.

The Chief taught me to live off the land, to harvest in traditional ways. And every time there was an act of harvest, an act of accessing a resource, Chief Tom Dawson would take a momentary silence. He gave homage to the Creator, thanking the Creator for the abundance we received. When we fished for salmon, he asked the salmon for protection, to be generous to us, and to be kind, because the salmon were our source of energy, of life.

———

A HEREDITARY Chief, like Tom was, like I am now, is someone whose lineage can be traced back to our Genesis. Hereditary Chiefs carry responsibility for our community; some of that responsibility is administrative, but much more of it is spiritual. My father would have been a hereditary Chief, had he not passed so early, so young. We hold the sacred; we hold the known and the unknown. We hold our stories. We bring people together and we help them to provide for our families as one.

Our Genesis stories, our Gilga'lis, are sacred, and it is here that I must share with you one of these stories, one that I know well. There are many versions, adaptations of these stories our Chiefs have shared with us that are enhanced by each community's own origin, by each Chief's way of explaining our earliest beginnings. These are stories that echo other ancient tales of beginnings, of great acts of bravery, and of the supernatural.

There were four wolves, three male and one female, who sat in the North. As the Great Deluge approached, they looked for a place of safety on the peak of Having-Phosphorescence, a great mountain. When the floodwaters finally drew back, the wolves were able to return to their lands.

The oldest of the wolves, named Listened-to, turned to his siblings and removed his mask.

To the others he said, "Take off your wolf masks. It is time to end our time as animals. From this point, we become human."

Listened-to, Healing-Woman, and their two younger brothers, Supernatural-One and Slow-in-house, therefore lived new lives. One day, as they sat together, Listened-to made a sudden and unexpected move. He grasped

Supernatural-One around the throat and bit his neck, leaving him dead. As his siblings looked on, the ancestors of all the tribes of the whole world, Listened-to then cut up his brother's body, and compressed the pieces into a ball, throwing it into the air as he spoke.

"Do not mourn your brother. In what I do next, we will increase our numbers. Watch!"

As the ball of brotherly flesh flew in the air, it transformed into eagle down. Each feather was taken up by the wind, blowing all over the world.

Listened-to spoke to the eagle down. "You will become human and you will become many. Our world will be populated by you."

Later, Listened-to moved to Kingcome Inlet, where Slow-in-house came to visit.

"My brother, Listened-to, will you tell me the songs of the birds here?"

Listened-to answered with the robin's tune. "Dzawadzali, Dzawadzali," he sang.

Slow-in-house responded, "Your people in this place will now be called the Dzawada'neux."

This gift of a name was repeated when Listened-to visited Slow-in-house at his home at Wakeman Sound. Slow-in-house whistled and chirped a lark's call, and the people in his village came to be called Haxwa'mis.

THE FIRST TIME I really observed Chief Tom Dawson, it was a night in the Big House, when he told stories deeply embedded in our language. He had a booming, powerful voice. And even as a little child, I could tell he was eloquent. He was resplendent in his best standards, his headpiece and the cedar bark around his neck, holding the Talking Stick. An impressive man.

One Potlatch, after telling his own Genesis story, he greeted the people, "Please listen to me, I have something to tell you."

"We are more than driftwood, all my relatives, Namwayut," Chief Tom Dawson said that night, pausing, and repeating his words. "We are more than driftwood. We have value. We have purpose, all of us in this sacred circle."

We all have a reason to be here, each of us, he went on to say. And it's up to each of us to discover what that is, so that it can keep us moving along life's pathway. We are all taking incremental steps: going forward, going backwards, sideways, being joyous, being sad, losing, winning, and somehow, in the sum total of all of that, knowing our purpose.

In fact, whatever has manifested at the end of your life, that is the sum total of your purpose. Finding that purpose is never over until our last breath, and that means we have to live every moment we can to the best of our ability.

Chief Tom Dawson had a reason to be here, starting with the way he led the Kwakwaka'wakw resistance to the Potlatch ban. I used to sit with him and some of his peers when I was little. Willie Seaweed, Chief Hilamas of the Nakwaktokw, and the great master carver Chief Herbert Johnson—these guys lived and breathed the old ways, the culture. They knew all the laws. And for some reason, they recognized that whatever the future held for our children, which meant people like me, it was going to be so difficult, so challenging.

"People are going to want to reject you and reject everything that we stand for. And we won't be here to fight your fate. And we're trying to tell you all these things, so that you can carry something for you, that will make a difference," Chief Tom Dawson would go on to say to us.

I learned that all Chiefs truly lead by inspiration and actual involvement. Their purpose was to determine how we would transition from full cultural existence to one that was underground. They figured out where we could secretly hold Potlatches, they would have sentinels along the Kingcome Inlet, and they would watch for people coming in: the authorities, the Royal Canadian Mounted Police, or we Indigenous.

But Chief Tom Dawson had another purpose, and that was mentoring me in addition to all of his own children and grandchildren.

His teachings were about how I should conduct myself. "When you work, you have to work hard," he told me.

You can't try to do it all at once, he would say, because you're either going to get hurt, or you're going to make a mistake. You've got to be steady. When you're tired, and even when you're beginning to be tired, you can rest. You can stop for a moment, take a deep breath, sit down, take it easy. And then after a few minutes when you get your strength back, you get back to work.

"Remember, always, who you are, that you're a good boy. And you have to respect people. You have to treat them well. You have to learn to listen. And, always, you've got to be paying attention. Because if you're not paying attention, you're not going to learn anything. Be respectful of people, and they will teach you."

He taught me how Creation was manifest, that it was all one—one Creation, one humankind, one Creator, and that what we learned spoke to the interconnectedness of everything. He would talk about a time when the animals and humans could talk to each other. He spoke metaphorically about the spirit world, to remember that there was just a thin veil between ourselves and the spirits around us, and that we were one with them. And he talked about the undersea kingdom alongside all of us, and that we had peace treaties with each other and with the whales. He was so apt at conveying those messages—of wholeness, of oneness, of balance and harmony, and for all of us needing to care for each other.

Chief Tom Dawson had a work ethic. He had humility. And a deep care for his family, for me, and for his own children who were older than me. He knew of things that were greater than ourselves. He found time. He spent time.

After I had been at residential school for five years, an official elementary school was built in Gwa'yi, and I was able to leave St Michael's and live in the village for two years before I had to return to the residential school in Alert Bay to begin high school. For these two years, even under the tutelage of the same sort of English, church-aligned scholars as at St Michael's, I came back to my family and myself, and I thrived. My Indian Affairs Branch report cards from that year, issued confusingly under the Department of Mines and Resources, show that I flourished at Kingcome Inlet Indian Day School, with high marks in Composition, Spelling, Science, Health, Grammar, and Reading, and even an A in Arithmetic.

Chief Tom Dawson's reason to be here, for me, was to teach me to remember my value. For a short time I knew who I was, and I felt safe.

———

WE MUST come back to ourselves.

When we speak about the human person, one individual, we can also see the context of all of humanity.

All of us individually, every person born, has value and purpose. We have to call in our own personal integrity in all the things that we do. That's when these become a core part of who we are. Understanding that purpose is the real way to end the division of hatred and racism, by creating a deep understanding that we bring about through dialogue. Often, we complicate this process by looking at our collective issues through one particular lens, and not realizing how steep a hill it is and how great a wall it is between us.

I think the first big mistake was that everybody thought that everything started in the new world, and by the new world, I mean Europe. People colonizing my home believed that they were superior, and that nobody else mattered. In fact, they likely believed that we must be eager to be transformed to a European way of life, and if they made all of us in their image, then there would be paradise, right? What we're discovering now is that we have to allow for all of us to be who we authentically are, with the languages we're born into, with the cultures and traditions and worldviews that we hold, and to come together and celebrate those differences and hold each other up. This is reconciliation.

When we seek our destiny, we also can be emboldened by the idea of our human value, and by the idea that the Creator lays out a purpose for all of us. In wrestling with the harm and loss of hatred and racism, somehow we discover that there are pathways forward. There were times in my life, as you will read in this book, that I didn't know what to do to survive, that I could not comprehend how to navigate the level of despair that I found myself in. But when I found myself remembering these messages, I realized that I had a responsibility to carry those messages forward.

Be respectful of people, and they will teach you.

Reconciliation is an ancient imperative. We can sustain the environment, the resources, the cultures, the rituals, and the ceremonies of us all. This is a well of rich history—of practice and tradition, values and ethics. And all we've got to do is open the door to all of those sources of knowledge, recognizing our value in all the different ways that we live. We've got to learn to live with ourselves first. Love ourselves first. Value ourselves first. And as we grow as individuals, we can become collectives. We can manifest a higher, larger value and purpose that gives hope and inspiration to nations of people.

And then, we are more than driftwood. We are an ocean.

(8)

BREATHLESS

I N GRADE eight, I was returned to Alert Bay, and my grief returned as well, but I hid it from Pat and the others the best that I was able.

For the most part, as we entered adolescence, we were still idle and bored. My schooling at Kingcome Inlet had done me well, and for the first few months back I was receiving accolades for my writing and oration skills, but my grades soon started to slip again as I felt the weight of distance sink me further into the enveloping darkness of abuse. We looked for ways to escape the monotony and never-ending hassles of residential school life. We were always trying to create ways to counter the harsh and brutal environment at St Michael's Indian Residential School.

Saturday was my favourite day. It was the one day that we could go on village leave without supervision. If we were lucky we would receive a small allowance if our parents had left a small deposit for us. Our leave would allow us to be off the school grounds between 1:00 and 5:00 pm, when the dinner bell would ring. When we were able to afford it, we could take in a movie at Pepper's Theatre in the Bay.

I loved movies. The first movie I ever saw was called *From Here to Eternity*, but Audie Murphy and Marilyn Monroe were my favourite actors. Movies with cowboys and Indians were also very popular, and on the playgrounds later, we would re-enact the personalities of our movie heroes. We never played the part of Indians.

Sometimes we would wander around if we had no allowance. Most times I would be with my brother, Pat. The very first time we went out together, when I was small, we were walking toward the white end of town, as it was called. This was the business district across the Indian/non-Indian divide, which began at the BC Packers Fishing Company with its cannery, net lofts, and wharves, as well as a huge store. During this era, BC Packers had a high fence that straddled the main road and sealed islanders off from each other at night. The first store after BC Packers was Mr Hall's General Store. Pat pulled me aside as we were approaching the store and gave a direct instruction.

"Pay attention, I'm giving you twenty-five cents," he said. "We are going into that store, and I want you to purchase bubble gum or candy," he added.

He instructed me to go to the counter and pay for what I had and then we would walk out together. Of course I followed his instructions without question. Pat was older than me and always seemed to know better. He was always looking after me. We exited Mr Hall's store and continued our walk. He pulled out a couple of comic books and other small items from inside the folds of his clothing and pockets. I had been a good decoy.

Later on in the afternoon we started making our way back to St Michael's. Sometimes the main street was littered with everybody's garbage. Bags here and there would be blown across the road. Pat made a point to look into every bag that we saw.

"Why are you looking into every bag that you spot?" I asked him.

"You'll see," he said tensely. As if by arrangement, he picked up a brown paper bag that had a twenty-dollar bill in it.

"See," is all he said.

From then on, I was trying to race him to pick up paper bags and look into them. I seemed to have lost any sense of embarrassment over doing that.

Pat and I would never stop looking out for relatives who might be in town. We were not allowed to make any house visits but occasionally we would sneak in a visit to people who were close to us. They would always share whatever they could with us because it was common knowledge that the food at St Michael's was a challenge. We'd also look for food on the wharves where there were all kinds of fishing boats tied up. In big salmon seasons there could be hundreds of boats moored. While these wharves were technically out of bounds for us, there was just no way to monitor the situation. Fishermen were making big money and were prone to be generous to poor wretches like us. They would give us loose change or invite us into their galleys to share a meal. On occasion boats were left open as crew members were uptown in the bars or shopping. We would help ourselves.

Sundays also provided a degree of relief when we had to attend church services at Christ Church. It was not so much that we were into worship or religion, but that we were able to be somewhere else other than the residential school. We would dress in our finest garb, which were our uniforms, and walk in a line down to the church. Sometimes we got there early and rushed right into the church ahead of the regular parishioners. Other times we would have to bide our time until everyone else was inside, and then we would file in as a group.

Wherever and whenever we went, we were always in public view. We were the object of much pity or scorn. It was a hard stigma to live by. Many saw us as poor unwanted children. It was no different for church people. But I loved the hymn singing and I did enjoy some of the Bible stories.

Then there would be the "collection" of money, as attendants would go from aisle to aisle with small handbaskets. Of course, none of the school students had anything to give so it was always slightly embarrassing. But attending that church did have meaning for me, even if I couldn't explain it.

Even so, while on Saturday leave at one point, Pat and I were walking by Christ Church and admiring it. We saw the beautiful white picket fence fronting the entire church property. It had recently been painted white, but one end of the fence was sagging. We edged to that section and rode the fence backwards and forward. All at once, like a ripple and a wave the entire fence collapsed. Pat and I hightailed it out of there.

One evening playing Indian baseball, I was excited to be included. The teams were made up of all of us— different ages and abilities. I was the youngest player on the field. I stepped up to the plate, and the pitcher was one of the bigger kids who threw really fast balls. His first two pitches swished by me as I swung helplessly, but on the third pitch I swung the bat aimlessly and managed to catch a piece of the ball. On instinct I dropped the bat and beelined for the marker.

My bad luck was that the pitcher had intercepted my hit directly. While I heard my teammates cheering in the background, running hard with my head down I looked up to see the pitcher winding back with his throwing arm. The next moment I felt the ball crash into the back of my head, and I was leaning over holding my sensitive ear, reverberating in pain. It stung so hard. I made a beeline for him, yelling threats about getting even. He stood his ground and braced himself. I was almost on top of him when he swung his right fist. The light seemed to flicker, and I observed the explosion of a magnificent array of stars. My teammates picked me up and took me to the washroom to clean myself up, and I stared into the mirror to see my first black eye.

———————

OUR EFFORTS to let go of our grief and pain and forget who we were became much worse than a black eye. In the burgeoning years as we moved through high school, everything became black.

One Saturday, while most of the boys' population was out on village leave, a small group of us stayed on the school property. It was a warm and sunny day, and we were all outside, and our supervisor had gone inside. We wandered aimlessly toward an old, abandoned tractor parked inside an open shed at the front of the hill near the barn. Someone had left it to rot and thought nothing of it.

One of the older boys looked furtively around to see if the supervisor was close by. Seeing no one else around, he climbed atop the tractor, removed the gas cap, and cradled the spout in his palms. He began sucking fumes from the gas tank as hard as he could. Finally, he rolled off the tractor to the ground, chuckling mysteriously. He was covered from head to toe with brown dust. He kept trying to stand up, only to fall over again. It seemed hilarious and we all laughed our heads off.

The boys coaxed me to do the same. I began to inhale the fumes, sucking as hard as I could. At first, I heard a loud and distant humming in my head. It felt strange but good, as if I wasn't there. Then I was falling, not able to control myself. I hit the ground with a thud, tried to get up but kept rolling over, much to the delight of the others. The world had started spinning and then it got dark, and I had tried to wake up, finding the world around me staggeringly wrong.

It was an extremely short buzz, then I got the worst headache I had ever experienced. Sucking gas was called "boo-hog," and we'd do it whenever we could find our way to the tractor without being noticed, because despite the pain it caused, the high provided an immediate sense of relief and escape from everything else around us: the hunger, the sexual and physical abuse, the name-calling, the cultural violence.

We found other ways to achieve the same high with the simplest of implements. Someone found a towel in the shower room and rolled it into a snake. We all took turns wrapping the towel around our necks and choking ourselves until we momentarily passed out on the floor. Sometimes we'd use leather straps. We blacked out right away without the oxygen we needed to breathe.

————

BY THE TIME I started to get a little older, I began to think about the things that triggered my anger and fear, but the violence I imposed was on myself.

At St Michael's, our Kwak'wala accents meant that we couldn't pronounce English words properly. There were and are no *s* sounds and *sh* sounds in our language. In grade nine, our school principal, Mr B, had called me to the head of the class in front of the blackboard and wrote the word "sugar." He asked me to pronounce it. I pronounced it wrong and he grabbed me by the shoulders and slammed me against the wall three times. This was the same principal who would deliberately trip his students in the hallway as an excuse for not paying attention.

By the age of fourteen, however, I was the one slamming myself down. The summer after ninth grade, I was hired by a relative to fish on a seiner. Fishing was lucrative but the weekends were long, and even though I had never had booze before, my friend Ed invited me to drink a full bottle of Lamb's Navy Rum with him. We wanted to be ready for a dance—a dance I never made it to because I was so drunk. We sat opposite each other in the fo'c'sle, passed the bottle back and forth along with a jug of water and drank it until it was empty. I jumped off my bunk, my head started swimming and I staggered and couldn't stand up. I told Ed to just go ahead. My first drink was the first time I passed out.

In Alert Bay, the hub of the North, hundreds descended upon the tiny community every weekend. Loggers, miners, fishermen, government workers, and people from outlying Indigenous communities would all come, but there was not much to do in Alert Bay except party. As a young crew member on a boat, living quarters were tight, so you would be in the village sooner or later being dragged into parties. By the end of that summer, I had developed the habit of overdrinking, and I did not know yet that my growing alcoholism was tied to my residential school experiences.

Having returned to St Michael's after that first fishing season, I heard Pat, who had already left the school, hollering from the porch of one of the homes close to the wharf. We had learned to track down not only food from the boats at the wharf, but also alcohol from the bootleggers all too willing to sell for our hard-won fishing money.

"Hey bro, come on in and have a drink!"

I said no, and that I was back in school.

He was insistent, so I joined him. My one drink turned into a few, and I suddenly realized that it was supper time at St Michael's and I needed to be there because I was a Table Captain.

I made my way back to the school and the dining room without detection. I was just starting to dish out food when I heaved with waves of nausea from the alcohol rushing through my bloodstream. All hell broke out and I was sent to isolation. Principal B was angry. He said he'd had enough of me and that I would have to see the Indian Agent to determine my fate. While the Indian Agent made nothing of the incident, the principal could not let it go. By grade eleven, I had added the habit of smoking cigarettes. Smoking was something that was largely ignored by the school's teachers because it usually took place far from the halls of the building, but Principal B decided to make an example out of me.

Principal B called a general assembly of all of the boys in the school, and placed a single chair in front of them; the students' eyes trained on that object in silence. The principal ordered me to drop my pants and kneel on the chair, bringing out a leather strap. I gritted my teeth in silence, willing myself not to cry as I was whipped over and over again on my bare buttocks and testicles.

It was humiliating, painful, and shaming, especially as I knew my pain was being witnessed by so many other children and young men as a message. They had to know their place. They had to know their bodies were subject to the whims and the beliefs and the desires of the white men and white women in this place, and in the world they controlled outside of the doors of St Michael's—the world on both sides of the white line dividing Alert Bay, the world farther away in Vancouver, across Canada, everywhere.

At the end of grade twelve, I walked down the steps of St Michael's Indian Residential School succumbed to the weight of oppression. How do you internalize the things you can't see or feel or touch or smell? How do you know that the weight has gotten too heavy to bear, or that the world can no longer be sensed? The "civilization" that had imposed itself on me told me the same messages over and over again.

You're no good.

You have no value.

You're just a pagan.

You cannot think for yourself.

God save the King.

God save the Queen.

Say your prayers.

Do the things we tell you to do.

Because that will make you better.

Two giant totem poles had guarded the entranceway to this school, this supposed home, and I left, walking slowly down those steps, under the shadows of the outstretched wings of two huge Thunderbirds.

The lights had gone out in the universe behind the mask, the stars in the sky, the waves of the ocean were silent.

And I was on my own.

And I did not belong.

(9)

SOMEWHERE LEFT
TO TURN

———

I HAD NO qualifications for anything when I graduated in 1958.

Just after graduation night, I felt free and optimistic, especially looking out at the fishing boats in the harbour. In Alert Bay, the season was set to boom once again, and my uncle Archie Robertson hired me as one of his crew on the *Cedric A*. We'd fix up the nets, paint the boats, haul supplies into the hold. The weather was holding, and in early August we were ready to set out. I wanted to untie the lines and take off in my uncle's boat, always turning around to take one last look at the school building protruding up higher than the net loft, higher than anything else. But we had a few more days of work to do first.

As we worked, we were living on the boats. When it was the last weekend at dock and we knew we'd be in close quarters for several weeks, we decided to have a party. Of course, there were hotels and bars left and right down the main street in Alert Bay, but, not having set out for the fishing season, we weren't looking to spend a lot of cash. With three of my friends, we grabbed some booze from a bootlegger and we went to one of their boats and drank, just sitting around a bunk.

Too soon, we ran out of the booze.

Instead of spending more money we didn't have, we decided to find another party. In some of the bigger boats (and there were quite a few preparing just as we were), we could see bottles being passed, we could hear the laughter, and we thought we'd fit right in. One of my friends pointed toward another seiner, and we all filed in.

It just happened so fast.

"All right, you guys, give us some of your booze," I said, edging up to one of the bunks, smiling.

I heard no response, but all of a sudden I felt a bottle smash on the top of my head, and looked up to see a guy sitting on the top bunk, leering down at me. He jumped, bolted out of the cabin and off the boat as I made an effort to strike back. He was fast. I jumped up, chasing him onto another boat. I saw him turn a corner and go down into the engine room. As I shifted around the engine room wall in the dark, he jumped me. This time he didn't smash my head. He cut my face with the broken bottle he was still carrying and left me there to bleed.

My friends had scattered, and I didn't blame them. I walked from the dock to the hospital with a big towel on my face, blood draining through to my hand. The physician on call was equally as inebriated as I was at that point, and I was wide awake as he was sewing up the wound, his hands shaking.

When I woke up in the hospital, I was covered in bandages. As I walked out the door, the secretary called out to me. My mother, my Ada, Sally, who had been diagnosed with cancer, was in that same hospital. I was sitting there getting stitched up the night before, bleeding because I had asked a stranger for free beer, and my mother was sick and dying with cancer. It broke my heart, and all I could do was walk right out the door. She had done everything possible to make my life better, invested everything she had to put my needs first. My grief, my pain, was too much to bear, and so I ignored it, ignored her grief and her pain, and just left to get on that boat and go fishing.

Weeks later, as we were coming back into the Bay from the fishing grounds at Johnstone Straight, I heard the chatter on the VHF radio. My uncle came down to the fo'c'sle.

"I hear that your mother passed away."

"Yeah," I said. "I hear that too," was all I could say.

It was the worst of all the things that had happened. Ada's passing just put a stamp on everything that had happened, every emotion that I could not bear to witness.

When we returned, we carried my mother to the Anglican Church at Kingcome village. The preacher, a big man with a beard, came up to us.

"You can't leave that in there. You've got to take that casket away from the church."

It didn't make sense. That's what everybody did. We always laid our loved ones to rest there before a funeral.

"Why not?" I asked him.

"Because I said so," he said, turning his back on us. "You can't leave it there, so find another place to put it."

We walked my mother's casket to our smoke shack. At first, I was angry. But then I thought maybe that was appropriate. She grew up in those places, smoking the salmon, preparing our community's food for the season. Those places are just as holy as a church.

I was angry for a long time. It took me quite a while to recognize the insanity of all that had happened. Those few weeks earlier, when I was in the hospital, a lot of people were outraged by my actions because I was known as a good boy, a boy who didn't get in fights. Even the principal of St Michael's came to visit me, urging me to press charges against the young man who cut my face, urging me to get out of his town and get an education—a real one.

After the fishing season I made the decision. I always wanted to be educated, I just didn't have a chance. But I decided to try one more time.

———

AT POWELL RIVER'S Max Cameron Secondary School, some of my teachers had told me I had a talent for language, for rhetoric, and there wasn't any reason I couldn't try to get a place at the University of British Columbia. In fact, for some reason unbeknownst to me, a few years earlier at St Michael's, I had skipped straight from grade four to grade six. It was the year before I was allowed to return to Kingcome Inlet for a short time. I was happy about that because it meant that I would attend class away from the residential school building at the Indian Day School, a separation from the suffocating dominance of the three-storey brick building with fewer staring eyes to monitor everything that we did. The wooden school building of the Indian Day School had mirrored army housing units, their former use, and there were more teachers as well. Even though my excitement was short lived, as Mrs S's authority would be exercised with the same heavy hand and strongly racist tendencies, it was academically a successful year, as illustrated in my report cards.

I was doing well at Max Cameron, or at least as well as I could be doing without making too much effort.

I had enrolled in a senior matriculation course there, commonly referred to as grade thirteen at the time, which was required if I was going to university. I stayed with Reverend Powell, who had been a resident priest at Gwa'yi for a few years. But my unresolved trauma only served to follow me there.

One Sunday morning, the reverend woke me from a deep, alcohol-induced sleep.

"Do you know the RCMP came knocking on our front door this morning? They left you a note," he said, handing it to me and leaving the room.

Bob, we have your convertible parked at the waterfront dock. Come and pick up your key at the detachment office and retrieve your car.

I didn't own a car, nor did I have a driver's licence. I was so embarrassed and ashamed; I went downstairs and told Reverend Powell that I was quitting school and returning home. That evening, however, he invited his best friends, Mr and Mrs Baxter, over for dinner to talk me out of it.

"Why do you want to quit school and leave?" Mrs Baxter asked gently.

My feeble response was that I felt out of place. I had no decent clothes, I said to her.

"But that's not a problem at all, we can buy you all of the new clothes that you need," she replied reassuringly.

My humiliation and false pride prompted me to say that my decision had already been made, and that I was leaving.

The next morning, a Monday, I walked across the street to the school to give notice and pick up my belongings. Mr Brown, my homeroom teacher, saw me entering the classroom. With a stern look, he started in on me.

"Bob, you're late again and you live just across the street. You have to do better."

I told him that he would never have to worry about me again, because I was leaving town. He stopped, looked at me puzzled, then stunned. He invited me out to the hallway and asked me to clue him in on what was happening. Mr Brown wanted me to seriously reconsider, but I simply thanked him for his caring ways and said that I had made up my mind. Tears welled up in his eyes as he said he was sorry to see me go.

These were good people who cared about me, who were loving, and I was inadvertently failing them, hurting them. Reverend Powell, Mr and Mrs Baxter, Mr Brown—I dismissed them all when they reached out to help. I was not able to see this kindness when it was extended to me, and I am sorry.

———

MY GREAT CHIEF and caregiver Tom Dawson, who had since been bestowed with the name Gwa-yum-gi, Monumental Whale, had become frail and went to live with his other family members, before passing away. I ended up couch-surfing for a while with different relatives. Sometimes I lived with my foster sister, Na'di. I would live with Aunty Pearlie or Uncle Tom. It was a challenging way to live and ate away at my self-respect and dignity. I started working in the logging industry, working at camps like Belle Isle, Charles Creek, and Wakeman Sound. That eased the pain a little as I would stay in camps for periods of time and feel better about being gainfully employed, going back home only on the weekends. Even at home, I took up any jobs that needed doing, and kept my head down. But I was still drinking, still trying to forget. For many years after leaving St Michael's, life blurred together as I moved from one job to the next.

When I drank alcohol, I felt a sense of freedom, and my cares were washed away for a time.

I made good money, and for several years this fuelled my addiction, but I would never achieve seniority in the unions because I would fail to show up for work, especially in the first five years after I had left the residential school. All of my work was attenuated by my need to quell the noise telling me that I would amount to nothing, that I was nothing.

Even in the safety of the village I loved, and with my connection to my family restored, I was ashamed of who I was. I thought back to the seventh grade, on my break from residential life, when I went home for lunch break from school every day. I had walked past the Big House where a Potlatch was unfolding. I heard the singing and glanced through the door and saw the dancing, and I felt shame sweep over me.

"Why are they still doing this?" I had asked myself, walking faster to get away.

They were celebrating because the Potlatch ban had been rescinded that year, and government officials no longer seemed to care about what Indigenous Peoples were doing in their own homes. Although St Michael's still operated a further twenty years, there was a trickle of change taking place.

My interest in my own culture and my own language, corrupted by the abuses I had faced at the school, created this feeling that continued to wash over me as an adult. It haunted me that I did not believe that I was capable of furthering my education and my own life.

———

I USED TO HEAR about the University of British Columbia—a place so glamorous, and so intellectual. When I was young, I wanted to be there, in that place, in that frame of mind, being somebody who could explore the mysteries of a different life, and it was only much later in my life that I was given the commission of an honorary doctorate degree there. Personally, in that moment, among all those brilliant students graduating, this was a special kind of triumph. I was different from everybody else in the room, but I was standing at a podium, knowing that we can triumph over whatever we face: adversity, hopelessness, pain. I knew that, in some way, I had become the teacher I had always wanted to be.

In that moment, I also reflected on our Indigenous ways of knowing.

In my earliest childhood, I understood that we all learned through the sculpting of our minds by our Elders. The old Chiefs who took on the speaker's role in their communities would tell us our origin stories, our Genesis, sharing the same words to us to remind us of what mattered, what was sacred, what bore repeating. They would speak to us at Potlatches, at the smoke shacks in November when we came together to gather the fish. They would speak to us when we were sitting around a fire taking the bones out of the smoked fish, or when we were drawn together for ritual. Somebody would take their time to unravel our family stories— our stories of events that changed us as a people. The speakers maintained this practice, their practice, and we, listening, had to pay attention. Anything we heard become clearly imbued in our minds, our brains trained by that repetition. We enjoyed it, but we were also doing the work of learning.

Once more my revered mentor Chief Tom Dawson whispers some thoughts from times past. It goes something like this: When the day is done and it becomes the past, learn all that you can. The new dawn, the new day is yours and what you do with that will be up to you. I think he was right. If we can do that, it creates a cradle of hope that can inspire and empower us.

When, one day, it was my turn to speak, I realized that I had no training. I thought about how our knowledge was passed down. And one of the first things I learned was to say something then repeat, repeat, and repeat.

In speaking, I learned my own story. Every step I took, every thought I had, every action I decided upon was of a purpose—was of that moment. Every story was the result of an accumulation of all the stories that have made up my life. Whether it was a failure or a success, I took on this responsibility to try to teach people about my life experience.

Your own story starts with you. Your story starts with you, but often, because you're so busy, you are likely to forget your own story. You may be trying to meet the next story. In doing so, you will have lost sight of all the things that have actually made you who you are. In doing so, you will have lost the ability to share parts of your story with others, the ways of knowing that matter to your children, your loved ones, your community.

I believe that everybody should keep a journal and use it as a tool to record their stories, reflect on these stories, and grow as a person. We should learn from ourselves.

And then, maybe once a year, or twice a year, or once a month, we need to set aside time to talk about our innermost values to the people we love.

The practice of telling stories is very natural. It is everyone's inclination to listen, to learn, and then to tell a story in return in their own way.

(10)

EMERGENCE

FELT WATER on my torso, deathly cold.

I don't know how I got there on the beach, how I ended up with the North Pacific washing over me, the cold shaking me awake.

I suddenly burst up out of the water, thinking that I was fully submerged in the ocean and this channel of water was sweeping everything away including me. It was hard to determine the flow of water because it seemed to be still yet flooding everywhere, foreboding and frigid. I tried to put words to what I was seeing but I couldn't. I could see the plovers skittering on the sand, the sounds of nature ringing in my ears. Nature seemed as though it was the antithesis to who I was, something born of my own isolation.

I could have drifted away from there in the narrow channel. I could have just simply drifted away like a piece of trash. Disappeared.

All of my hard work had disintegrated because I could never sustain my belief in myself. As I succeeded, and even excelled, at a job, I would let it slip away. I would quit before the imposter me was found out. I had degenerated into a really hard-drinking, careless, risky-lifestyle person. There were so many blackouts in my life, extended periods of blackouts, that I don't know how I retained my brain cells. It had gotten that bad.

And one night, I was back in Alert Bay. We had started drinking, and I say "we" because there were a number of us, but I can't even remember who was there. It had been a typical, normal weekend in Alert Bay, where many of us were drinking too much. And it wasn't just us, the Indigenous, who kept ending up there. There were others who came to that community by the hundreds every weekend: fishermen, miners, loggers, transients, people from surrounding villages. It was just a cocktail of chaos. We did what we always did and got some bootlegged booze at the door of the pub and ran through the bush across the road from the RCMP. Somehow I had gotten to the beach on the other side of the island. It was at the end of a road under the reserve on Cormorant Island, isolated. The road goes right to the water's edge.

That night, I could not, did not, remember who I was. I did not remember what my purpose ought to be, even though I knew that something was still terribly wrong.

I had not yet reached rock bottom, but I was edging close to it.

As I lay on that beach on Cormorant Island only a few months after dropping out of school for the last time, I was so angry and so out of control. All of the things that happened to me because of my anger, I never considered how I was going to move beyond those emotions through forgiveness. And so I found myself almost drowning on a lonely stretch of beach. And it was not the only time. Another time I found myself there with a rifle, ready to pull the trigger on myself.

What I discovered was that I had to figure out how to let all of that pain go. I thought that I had to find some degree of forgiveness, or I was going to die.

I didn't want to die.

I began to understand that forgiveness starts with self. I began to understand that I'd better forgive myself for all the things that had happened to me, and the pain that I had taken on, and that I had blamed myself for, for whatever reason. I began to understand that I had to let it go. Little by little, bit by bit, piece by piece, I asked myself why I was responding in that way, why I was drinking too much, why I was getting hurt.

It was self-hate in overtime, and I realized that it was killing me.

I realized that I don't *have to* do something about it; I *get to* do something about it. Even when I didn't know what to do about it, I could pray for myself: Let me understand more and let me not be angry anymore.

And then it came to me, those words that Chief Tom Dawson spoke in the Big House gathering. *We are more than driftwood.*

I was, quite physically, almost a piece of driftwood, floating there in the ocean. Almost whisked away into the seafoam like nothing, without value, without purpose.

———

I HAVE no doubt that what I was experiencing, others were as well. For me, the time was still not right. I was still not aligned with my purpose.

It was around this time that I also felt the call to wonder why my birth mother had never taken me back. I knew that, near the end of her years, she worked at the Nanaimo Indian Tuberculosis Hospital, and later, at the Nanaimo General Hospital only a few blocks away, and I was overwhelmed with gratitude when she finally reached out: We would have real discussions and get to know each other. We would have a real relationship and she could answer all the questions I had about my father, and how we were placed with family. I could ask why I was left with Ada.

I made my way down the island to Nanaimo from Campbell River, following a forty-five-minute float-plane ride from Kingcome Inlet. I knocked timidly on her apartment door.

"Who is it?" she shouted.

"Me?" I responded with a raspy, dry throat.

The door swung open, and she said, "Come in, come in." We hugged each other for what seemed like a long time. We sat around her kitchen table for some time just talking. It was wonderful, and for that moment I felt whole.

She interrupted our discussion without warning.

"I want to show you something," she said as she quickly got up and turned to walk into another room, returning with a small box in her hand filled with papers.

"These are all the letters that you have written to me, my son, and I have kept them all. They are my treasures," she said.

I picked up a few of the letters, touching my own careful handwriting, knowing that she had read them but that she did not know what to do with her emotions, her regrets, her fear of feeling inadequate. I looked at the box in which they were kept, her own practical box of treasures there in that kitchen. Knowing that she was so close to me, but distanced by disease, circumstance, and the forced alienation between families that had become normal and expected in our time. We both cried a little and talked into the night.

The next morning I got ready to leave, feeling calm and content.

"Mom, can I come visit you again?" I asked.

Without hesitation, she hollered, "Yes, yes, please. And this time don't wait for a long lifetime to visit."

I made my way back home to Kingcome village, but only a few weeks later, when we were out towing logs, the sound of the VHF was again a cry of mourning, just like it was when Ada had passed. I heard the news that my mother had been killed crossing the street in Vancouver. It had been a dark, stormy night with high winds, heavy rain, and no visibility. Every bone in her body had been broken.

———

THESE BARRIERS we create within ourselves are both complicated and simple. It should be simple enough to act, to mitigate harmful things in the world. It should be simple enough to reconcile ourselves to our purpose. Forgiveness becomes a huge part of this process.

But we all think that forgiveness has just one meaning, and that's where we get in trouble.

Most people think that forgiveness is looking at the perpetrator of a transgression and saying to ourselves, I'm going to forget what they did, right now, and I forgive them. I was trying to forgive and forget my tormentors at St Michael's Indian Residential School. The World Council of Indigenous Peoples was trying to forgive and forget colonizers around the world and build a collective wisdom. Even the Department of Indian Affairs was hiring innovators like Professor Farrell Toombs, to forgive themselves for their past transgressions against us and forget what really happened.

When we forgive, we must do it for our own peace. In doing so, however, we may never forget what happened.

It would be a few years before I would work with George Manuel of the Secwépemc People. He created the World Council of Indigenous Peoples in 1972 when I was still working with the federal Department of Indian Affairs alongside him. I watched as, in addition to assisting the tribe, he also worked to increase wider awareness in the government and society of the problems and conditions faced by our people. He was one of the great leaders of all time. He was so brilliant, and not afraid. A courageous visionary, he and I happened to be working in the same role at the time. His stature in our community was huge. He was very well known. He was a warrior. I was just starting off.

George Manuel told me that we could gather the wisdom of all the Indigenous cultures, because nothing was more powerful than recreating our universal wisdom. At the first World Council of Indigenous Peoples gathering in Port Alberni in 1975, George knew that I did some writing, and so I was invited to tag along and report on what was discussed. But while much was accomplished, I was also shocked at the barriers we were creating. With all of the Indigenous leaders from around the world in the room, they started out by arguing about whether the Saami, from Finland, qualified for inclusion, even though their children had likewise been taken to residential missionary schools and had been affected by a legacy of laws that were created to deny their rights. Serenely planned meetings were almost always breaking out into fistfights.

We are all, at times, afraid of our own ability to take on our purpose. We are all, at times, worried that we might drift.

We must all stay the course because it's worth it. Even if it hurts a little while we stay the course, we must. If we cross that line, we are giving a little bit of ourselves away.

There are times when we all can find a really quiet place. A place where you can't hear your phone, movies, or others' voices. That is a place between you and your Creator, or just you and your conscience. That is a time when you can have a really good chat about what matters to you, to your integrity. If you're fortunate enough to have a Creator or a conscience, and you recognize what matters, then courage overcomes fear. When you're in the right frame of mind and intention, courage always overcomes fear.

Sometimes, as I found in my early days of adulthood, we think we don't have that courage. But what I know now is that we all do. In fact, each of us possesses the gifts that kings and queens and princesses or heroes or superheroes have. We all have the courage to stand our ground in that moment and even take one step forward. If, even in that one millisecond, we can hold that moment of courage, we can grow.

Like everything else, our integrity does not happen overnight. We work at it. Sometimes for a very long time. I still have lots of fears. Most of them are about my value in this world—if I matter. And the only thing that keeps me afloat is recognizing that I have the ability to stand my ground. I'm still standing like a rock. Knowing that is better than giving weight to those things that arise in my darker thoughts.

———

AS I lay on that beach on Cormorant Island, it would be some years before my vision on the fishing boat, when I heard the words from the Creator that I was loved, when my path began to truly shift and I found myself leaving the bottle behind forever. Even though I had learned that I needed to ask for help that day on the beach, it was not until I saw myself in the mirror of my wife's eyes, leaving with the children, that my heart opened to hear that voice.

I saw that constellation in the sky, and in that millisecond all of my experiences flowed together in a single point of light. Like a child in the Potlatch, I saw behind the veil and through the eyes behind the mask.

The force, the Creator, was reaching down and lighting that last ember in me, somewhere.

I was not done. I was not done yet.

In spite of what I had done to myself, I was a part of all of this and I was loved.

Culture can speak to a common humanity. We are all mortal, and, if we are lucky, we have access to the other dimension of the spirit world. But at the end of the day, we exist in our stories, our narrative of our human selves.

When we hear each other's stories, it is not only a deeply human experience, but we are also changed, transformed. Our consciousness deepens a little through what we know and learn about each other, and even if we don't take it all in, don't understand everything in that very moment, our hidden cognition is still processing everything in the background.

In the Potlatch, our ceremonies were intended to be highly theatrical, dramatic, and visual. But there were also subliminal messages communicated to us between everything that we saw and felt and heard and touched and smelled.

The same is true for our lives. What we do, watch, and feel is not the whole story. We start with the story we are told, and we tell ourselves the same story. But our minds are still working toward that purpose, that set of values that alights our commitment to ourselves and to the way that we belong to a group of people. The universe, so to speak, in its noble and mysterious ways, continues to touch our soul to bring us into alignment.

You are not done. You are not done yet.

(11)

THE DEEP

———

OMING FROM a place of deep longing to be seen and known, and to make changes I could not yet imagine into being, still barely into my twenties I decided to run for council in the village—a village of only twenty-one voters. Councils were the official organizational bodies in our villages. According to the Indian Act of 1876, a band could have one elected Chief and one elected councillor for every one hundred band members, with a minimum of two councillors required per band. Even with our very few voters, band councils were responsible for everything: the governance and administration of band affairs, including education, band schools, housing, water and sewer, roads, and other community businesses and services.

In our election, there was only one person who didn't vote for me, and this bothered my fragile ego. I spent the next day or two after the election visiting all the voters I knew. I elicited, one way or another, how they voted. Each of them told me that they had voted in my favour. The last person I approached was my own foster sister, Na'di.

I went to her, and I said, "You know, somebody didn't vote for me and it really bothers me a lot."

"It was me," she said.

"Why didn't you vote for me?" I asked.

"Stupid," she called me. "Because I didn't want you to get hurt."

In my heart, I understood what she meant. But things moved more quickly than I anticipated on this tiny council. In one of our meetings, the Indian Agent came in and joined us.

"Have you ever thought of doing anything else with your life, Bob, other than fishing and logging?" the Indian Agent asked me. "I've got this brochure," he said, handing me a piece of paper. "It's called community development, that's what the job is. It's part of Indian Affairs."

"Interesting. Well, leave it with me. I'll read it later, let you know," I said, having no idea what he was talking about.

I read it, and still did not fully understand what community development was. I left the brochure on the table for a few weeks before I filled it in and sent it out in the post. I had fully forgotten about the job when I got a call to come to Vancouver for an interview.

The interview was strange. They asked me about the weather back home, how the children were doing in the village, how I was feeling. No one seemed to bother asking me about what I thought about community development or my interest in it.

After about forty-five minutes, the agent said, "Yeah, you got the job."

Everything moved so quickly. In a very short period of time, they had shipped me off to Laval University in Quebec for a sensitivity training course. I didn't know what sensitivity training was, and neither did any of my eighteen peers in the classroom. Professor Farrell Toombs, who ran the program, didn't clarify why we were there, either. The professor left us alone for the first three whole days of class. He said nothing, he did nothing, and, in fact, he simply wasn't there. We'd all be reporting to class, but inevitably would arrive to an empty classroom of just us, the students. Somebody would make a paper airplane, and we'd watch it ride the air on its flight to the middle of the classroom.

Finally, Professor Toombs showed up.

Somebody stood up and said, "Mr Toombs, we're really disappointed. We're here to learn and yet there's no one here to teach us."

He gracefully didn't take offence.

"I wanted you to learn, first of all, that when you're assigned to a community, there'll be nobody there to tell you what to do. And you better figure out whatever your response is going to be fast. Otherwise, you're probably going to be out of there. That's your first lesson."

I understood what he was saying, but underneath my own façade, I was so confused. In the evenings, we'd all be drinking heavily. All of the students, flown in from across Canada, had the same background I had. We were supposed to be at Laval for three months, and I didn't know how I could handle it.

I was half-cut, right there in the classroom. Professor Toombs asked me what was going on.

I said, "I don't want to change. I don't want to change. I don't want to be here anymore."

"I'm not trying to change you," he said. "I'm actually trying to work with you to make sure that you *don't* change."

I was taken aback. Professor Toombs presented me with a different view on who I was, on my value. In his eyes, we mattered. I mattered. And it was something I needed to feel in my soul. Subconsciously, I didn't want to lose myself. I didn't want to lose who I was behind the façade I had created: that bold, alcohol-fuelled false self that had the guts to talk back to a professor; the false self I had learned to cultivate the last few years at St Michael's. Even though my actions meant that I was losing myself already to a large degree, something in me was fighting back.

When I came back from Laval University, I started to begin to resolve to be authentic, to be myself, to be

Kwakwaka'wakw, to hold true to the values that emanated from an ancient culture. My mind started to shift; the Potlatch began to take on some real significance in my mind again. I took on the mantle of my new role in community development seriously.

I had heard all the activists at Laval talk about Saul Alinsky. A community development expert, he was quoted in books and newspapers, and I wanted to be like this guy. He always carried a flip chart everywhere he would go when he went into communities. So, when I came back from Laval, I bought this really nice flip chart in a case, and I thought I had made it.

I was placed at a big reserve when I got back west, and I went to my first council meeting. I still hadn't figured out what I was doing there, despite the flip chart. I sat and listened to the council's stories, and those of the old Chief.

This beautiful, beautiful Elder was talking to his council and said, "I don't know whatever happened to us. In the old days, we had lots of fertile, rich soil. In the old days we used to grow all of our own food. We would go hunting in the bush. There would be people fishing down at the lake and the river. And now look at us, we're here, we're writing these welfare cheques and nobody goes to work anymore."

I went home that night, and I was mute. I thought about what he said. It was then that this idea was born to me, that community development had to be done in a way that empowers people to be *in* their own power, to control their own future, to do their own work.

————

THE VOICE that had uttered, "I don't want to be here anymore" in Laval did not go away.

I had married my wife on April 11, 1963, and I left the community development job I had once loved. We lived in Vancouver for a while. When I arrived in the city, I did not hear one word of my language, ever, ever, ever. Nor did I want to speak it myself. I would tell my wife not to speak our language. These people might hear us, I would tell her. I was just so afraid of repercussions.

At the same time, I was never afraid to take jobs I was not qualified for, because I knew that I would take on whatever challenge I faced. There was a juxtaposition between what I felt like inside and what I presented to the world. Three years after starting out in my community development role, I had come to Vancouver to work at the Friendship Centre. There were new people developing new ideas about what it meant to be Indigenous, and it was exciting. I took on a role as the program director and worked with young people, helping them find their own voices. But eventually, after about two or three years, the pressure got to me, and my drinking set in again. I entered into a pattern of imposter syndrome fits and starts, where I would achieve a goal and then let the shame wash over me until I had no recourse but to move inside myself.

It didn't seem that way on the outside; I was never fired from a job. One of the directors of the Board of the Friendship Centre, an old newspaperman, approached me.

"You know, I've been reading your reports for our board meetings," he said. "You're a good writer. Have you ever thought about writing for a newspaper? You should. I'll tell you what I'm going to do. I'm going to call the managing editor of *The Sun* and tell him you're going to come and talk to him."

Six months later, I happened to be on Broadway, right by the offices of the *Vancouver Sun*. I wandered in and I went up seven floors, opened the door, and the young lady asked me if she could assist me.

"Yes ma'am," I said. "I want a job."

She looked at me strangely and asked me if I had an appointment, and I said no, of course.

She said, "You can talk to the managing editor," and pointed at a man in an office with a view overlooking the vast mountains behind the city. I could see him through the door as she walked over to get his attention.

As I entered, Bill Galt walked over.

"You want a job?" Bill asked.

"Yes, sir."

"Do you know how to type?"

"No, sir."

"Have you ever written a story?"

"No, sir."

"Very interesting. I'll tell you what," he said, "I'm going on a vacation for two weeks. Come back here in two weeks and you can have a job."

In two weeks, I came back, not knowing what to expect.

"We're going to start you on the Indian beat," the city editor told me, using that archaic and frustrating term.

"No," I said.

"No? Well, what do you want to do?"

"I don't want to write about Indians until I know how to write."

"Yeah. Okay. I'll show you to your desk and I'll figure out where you can start."

He gave me a hand and some hints on how to start for my first assignment, how to prioritize my ideas so that I could meet a deadline, and what questions to ask. The who, what, where, when, why, and how questions. For the first few months, I reported to other writers on their beats, but I slowly got assigned to bigger pieces of my own.

One day, I was assigned to cover Lionel Hampton at Isy's Supper Club. I was told what to do, where to be, and when. It was going to be a real scoop, and there was a huge scrum outside of the club. I listened to the questions the other journalists were asking, and I jotted down the answers in my notebook. It went on for about twenty-five minutes, and finally, everybody left. And before I turned to go, Mr Hampton came up to me.

"Can you come with me for a moment?" he asked.

We went into the washroom and he took me aside conspiratorially.

"I just really want you to write a good story," he said.

"I'm gonna break the best story I can," I told him.

Then he took out his wallet and he peeled off some money.

"I want you to have this."

"I can't, sir, I'm working," I said, looking him in his pleading eyes. "Can't do it."

"Well, it's just a gift," he said. Hampton's fame was past its peak; he was still performing old hits, but he wasn't breaking new ground.

"No, I can't take it, but I'm going to do the best story I can on my first assignment on my own."

I don't know why he targeted me. It might have been my impoverished look. I have no idea, and I never did ask him. But I was the first Indigenous reporter ever hired by *The Sun*, and my integrity meant something to me.

I held values that I could not, at the time, have verbalized.

Integrity is real. It is the only thing that I own. Nobody else owns it, my integrity, and there might be some days when it's all I've got. I knew then that I could not surrender it or compromise it or give it up because it was my last stand against whatever would become of me without it. Integrity was and is the last little voice inside that tells you that you're crossing a line.

And with that, I knew that there was something inside of me that was pure—that had not yet been tapped.

———

WHEN I WAS beginning to emerge into myself, I thought that all of these jobs were a fluke—that they were beyond my control because I didn't have much control. I was going with the wind. But I realize now that I was welcoming all of these experiences.

Your purpose is already predestined before you are born. When we think about our purpose, we may mould ourselves to it or we may fight it. When we fight who we are, then we're not aligned with the purpose we have on this Earth.

Working in Vancouver, working in remote communities, the experiences that drew me close to my purpose were those that I solicited. In determining what each community wanted to know, I started to discover what I needed to know to help them, and to help myself. I listened to the elected people, the ordinary people, the grandmas and grandpas, and the young men and women, any people. Sometimes I was in an uncomfortable position because I was coming up against the powers that be. But my job, whether I was writing, or attending meetings with the community, or talking to youth, was to inspire people to think outside of the box so that they, too, could empower themselves in their own ways. So that they, too, could influence their own life and the lives of people they care about. And all my experiences were incremental to one another and helped me broaden my perspective on what I knew about the world around me.

At the same time, even as I honour what I have done, I know that my life was lived trying to make up time for myself, to make up time for everything that happened in my past.

We too, as one, have to make up time.

I feel like we are on the verge of a massive shift because, as of today, the average Canadian has now realized the situation when it comes to Indigenous communities is untenable. The climate situation is untenable. The hate we carry is untenable. The big auto industries and oil companies, in their current practices, are untenable.

All of these mediums are starting to converge. The whole map of man's inhumanity to man, and the need for reconciliation in Canada, are one and the same. We're going to have to change; we're going to have to do things differently. Challenges have been here for a long time that we've afforded to ignore, but there is much that we can do in our generation, our lifetime. Coretta Scott King said it best when she offered up the idea that freedom is never really won. Every generation has to struggle for its own freedom.

As long as we can allow our purpose to unfold, and not fight against it, our freedom can emerge.

The purpose we have here on Earth lives within us.

Me as a young reporter at the
Vancouver Sun. *Photo: Ray Allan*

Above: My first Gilford Island Potlatch in 1981; I am in the white sleeves on the left, watching people dance and honouring them by being present and standing.

Facing top: My wife, Donna Joseph, dancing to honour little children at our first Potlatch on Gilford Island (1981).

Facing bottom: In the front row, my cousin Dorothy Speck on the left, Na'di to the right, Vicki Dawson wearing a wolf mask representing the first ancestor, and Elsie Willams (1981).

Above: My son Bob, in the middle of the photo, doing his inaugural Hamatsa dance. Ernie Willie, my friend who did the Hamatsa in his youth, is directly behind Bob's head (1981).

Left: My son Bob, Na'di, my daughters Karen and Shelley, and my son Farrell.

Facing top: My son Farrell, dancing the Nułamała, the role of the guardian over the happening (1981).

Facing bottom: My daughter Shelley, the ghost dancer— the dance that belonged to my granny. The wooden skull she is wearing looks much more grotesque in real life.

Facing: Standing for the forest and its protection in the Sitka Valley. *Photo:* Vancouver Sun

Above: Fred Kelly, former National Chief Phil Fontaine, and me at the opening of the *Down from the Shimmering Sky* exhibition.
Photo: Adam Timrud

Former Prime Minister Kim Campbell and me at the opening of the *Down from the Shimmering Sky* exhibition. *Photo: Adam Timrud*

(12)

OUR WOMEN AND GIRLS ARE SACRED

HAD MARRIED the girl next door fourteen years before I stopped drinking.

At St Michael's, I had prayed so many times to find someone to love and to marry, someone with whom to have many children. I wanted to make sure I was never lonely again, and believed that if I could marry, my partner would be mine forever.

In Gwa'yi, I didn't notice Donna early on, but she was always nearby. She also attended residential school for a short while, but as the girls were in many ways separated from the boys at St Michael's, we often only passed each other in the halls. But by the time we had left the school, Donna had blossomed into a beautiful and radiant young lady. We fell head over heels in love with each other and exchanged vows within a few years of my returning home.

I was totally unprepared for marriage and what it meant, and I soon discovered that blind love was not enough to sustain us.

Donna was strong, bold, and resilient. Our oldest boys, Bob Jr and Frank, were born while we were still living in the village, and conditions were rudimentary. There was no electricity and no indoor plumbing, so Donna would pack drinking, washing, and cooking water from the Kingcome River, some hundred metres away. She would clean soiled diapers and bedding in bare feet, even on cold days, and when I was away at camp, she would chop wood and make kindling. She would wash the boys in tubs which first had to be filled with water she boiled on the wood stove. Perishables like butter, milk, and meat were placed in a wooden box outside the kitchen window. We eventually owned a motorized wringer washer, but Donna still had to dry clothes on lines outside and racks inside. There were few distractions like television; we had radios with good reception, the higher you strung the area wires on trees. Neighbours visited neighbours and families kept in close contact. We played cards and games like Monopoly and Yahtzee.

We seemed content until booze raised its spectre, time and time again. Then all of our ghosts from the past would reveal themselves. Unresolved trauma, anger, and dysfunction would test and strain our relationship.

We both worked outside of the home, and even as we went on to have our five children, Donna worked hard to support her family and children as well as her own siblings who had their own struggles and needed her support. She was tenacious and driven, holding jobs to make sure everyone was safe. She was a Native Court Worker for many years, and then worked as an executive director for two distinguished safehouses for women. She was an instructor in a Kwak'wala preschool. During one busy Christmas season, she took on extra work at the Vancouver Post Office. Occasionally Donna worked as a hotel chambermaid, and even found work in a car detailing shop. Nobody worked harder than she did.

———

MY WORLD collapsed when my wife left me with our children in 1975. Like everything else, I was not ready for the demise of our whole family. Those days were my darkest hours, and I have never felt so much pain in my life. I did not know whether I wanted to live or die, and I had ideations of suicide.

After my vision, and the realization that the ghosts haunting us needed to be quieted, and with alcohol left behind, Donna and I worked hard to reconcile. We did get together for a while after that, but it was not meant to be.

For a few years, I was single parenting, taking care of our children on my own. I would see the sadness in my children's eyes, and it would tear me apart. I would see their confusion, the bewilderment, as they fought the idea that their mother was somewhere else, not in our home. It wasn't their fault, and they didn't understand.

I lived with the remorse and regret every day, feeling that I had failed them as a father, that I could have done something to make Donna stay. It was hard to live, knowing their innocence had been betrayed, that they had to face their futures without her daily presence. Whenever I was out of sight of them, I would cry, especially at night. Within the darkness of my bedroom, I would shed tears for them. I really wasn't sure what to do anymore to respond to their pain and grief. I couldn't think clearly because it was so painful to look into their eyes and broken spirits.

I had to do something, but what I needed was outside help and advice. Alex lived behind my yard in a cul-de-sac bordering my property. He had become a good friend of mine, as we continued to bump into each other while attending the same self-help group. I was up early one morning and called Alex and said I was coming over. I climbed over my back fence, knocked on his door, and smelled the strong coffee brewing as I entered his house. I told him about the dark place I was in, and that I didn't know how to handle the predicament that I had placed my children in. Alex listened.

"Just talk to them, Bobby, and then listen. In fact, listen more than you talk," Alex said when he had heard all that I had to share. "It's no different from AA. You gotta get it out. Better out than in."

It felt like Alex and I had chatted for some time, but I made my way back home before the kids got ready for school. I woke them up, and they still all had the same sad eyes and seemed to be calling for something, anything. We finished breakfast, and I told the kids they all had to be home for dinner because I had an important announcement to make.

I spent the day in quiet contemplation and felt better than I had in a long time, eager for the kids' return. The children ate quietly as usual. At the end of dinner, just before the children dispersed, I asked them to pay attention.

"Everyone, listen up now. I know how hurt all of you have been because Mom is not here. I'm very, very hurt as well. I know how much you miss your mom. And I miss her, too. It hurts every day. And I can see you crying. Sometimes I cry too when I'm alone. We have to help each other work our way through this. We have to talk about it to understand and to let go of some of the hurt. So, from now on, after dinner, we will stay for a while at the table to do that. Let's start this evening. You will all say something to share. Share how you are feeling. Anything at all will be a good start."

Their sad little eyes said it all. They were confused, lonely, and deeply hurt. They needed that bit of prompting. But, in that moment, all the kids spoke ever so briefly.

When it was over, I breathed relief over this small breakthrough. We would be talking to each other as a family. My hope was that the children and I would feel reconnected, less lonely, and each in our own way, understand that we were supporting each other. I believe it was the first hard lesson to learn: how to communicate and foster dialogue so that we would all grow together and get past the despair of the moment. Dialogue and understanding are critical for families, as it is for reconciliation.

During these times I had to develop the practice of being prayerful, thanking the Creator for my friend Alex, thanking the Creator for good people everywhere, and thanking the Creator for my wife. Our last undeniable commitment to each other was to continue to be the father and mother of our children in every way.

I have kept that promise. We have kept that promise.

Ironically, and in a funny sort of way, Donna and I are together again in our old age living with our children. So much water has flowed under the bridge and we are a family. As a family, we are still finding ways to reconcile with each other. Apologies have been prompted in all the right moments, where they can be found. Forgiveness is a force of its own, as we have

learned to heal and renew and nurture our relationships. Prior to our breakup, my relationship with my
children was shaped by the forces of fatherhood and
my lived experience. In spite of all of my limitations
and shortcomings, I knew that my children loved me,
but as they have been growing and evolving through
their own lived experiences, they have forgiven me
little by little. They have become their own selves and
have grown up to be beautiful human beings, each
of them in their own way, with personalities focused
on giving back and contributing to a higher sense of
humanity.

––––––––

WHAT HAS ALSO emerged from our finding ways to
reconcile with each other as a family is a deep acknowledgement of the challenges that are faced by women
and girls, both within Indigenous families and communities, and within all families and communities.
The traumas faced by women today are not unlike
the impacts of residential schools and forced assimilation; I feel a parallel between my own experience
and those of many women I know and have known.
Violence through physical and sexual abuse is horrific
and debilitating, but the emotional violence with which
most women contend at home, at work, and in the
community can be just as devastating. All women face
incredible, overlapping challenges, as have my wife and

my daughters. Many of these challenges are unseen, not listened to, disrespected.

And yet women simply carry on in their strengths.

Women and girls are the very Cradle of Life. Women are our civilizations. They are the life givers, whether or not they bear children. They are the nurturers of ideas, values, and people. They are the instincts that manifest unconditional love, unconditional life. They are the caregivers. They teach, mentor, and lead our younger generations by example. They are the truest of role models.

It is time to restore women and girls to their dignified status, rightful status, and the rightful place and space they should hold in our communities.

And yet, in Indigenous communities, we know that there are missing, broken, and murdered women who are not being seen, who were never heard or treated as precious, and whose pain has been ignored for too long. The Highway of Tears is a 725-kilometre span on Highway 16 between Prince George and Prince Rupert, BC, where many Indigenous women have been taken from over the last fifty years—lost to murder, lost to disrespect, lost from our embrace. They are the recipients of violence at home and violence in our colonized land. Little by little, we lose our women and girls every day. It is our heartbreak when our women experience heartbreak. It is our pain when they suffer pain. We become powerless when women are powerless, and we must not pass this trauma-based pattern down to future generations.

When women are not loved, will this not diminish the love in us?

Unless we put a stop to this violence, we will be caught in an unrelenting cycle of trauma that will continue to destroy individuals, families, and nations. The violence must stop. The violence must end.

So where do we start? We start by acknowledging the problem. We start by educating each other about it. We start by taking responsibility. We do this by taking action.

Women and girls are precious. They are love personified.

They must be loved.

They must be honoured.

They must be revered as leaders.

Women are the great cornerstones and foundations of who we are, together. Without them, there is no future. Without women, who will build and hold our families together? Who will build our relationships in our communities? Who are we without the leadership of women? Why are we even here?

We must break the silence about the lived experiences of women.

We must talk about these experiences to seek collective healing, but even more than that, we must empower women and girls to speak their truths. We must empower women and girls to speak our truths. When we do this, we can confront our unresolved grief and trauma just as my own family has had to do. When we do this, we can begin to break our bonds to chronic sadness. Without breaking the silence, unresolved trauma, including historic, intergenerational trauma, will continue to impact us all.

Trauma must be addressed mentally, emotionally, physically, and spiritually.

That's why I vigorously support the Moose Hide Campaign, a grassroots movement of Indigenous and non-Indigenous men and boys who are standing up against violence toward women and all children. It is critical, as this campaign calls for all men to heal ourselves so that we can teach our young boys about the true meaning of love and respect, and be healthy role models for them.

The trauma experienced by women must all be confronted. We must bring this message home to our friends and neighbours; we must talk about it in our homes, around kitchen tables, and in our schools. We must address it where we live, work, and play. It requires everyone's effort and support.

It starts today.

(13)

OPENING THE BOX

—————————————

THE LAST official Potlatch, after the 1884 federal ban, was held in 1921. Chief Dan Cranmer flouted the law at his home on Village Island, 'Mim'kwamlis, but the RCMP found out and raided the place, and forty-five people were arrested, mostly high-ranking, and asked to surrender their masks and their blankets if they wanted to avoid prison. This regalia was seized by the police and sent to museums in Ottawa, the United States, and Europe. That same year, following the raid, all Indigenous Peoples were forced to take on an English name and register it with the government. We did not exist to the government until we became the Josephs, the Dawsons, the Scows, the Hunts, the Cranmers—until we had rejected the names we gave ourselves. Oral history tells us that we simply chose our names out of an English book that was passed around our village, or that we were given our names by the Indian Agent or through intermarriage.

At the same time that I began to remember Chief Tom Dawson's words to me, I also began to return to the Potlatch.

Some of my friends had told me that they needed my help in revitalizing Kwakwaka'wakw culture. The return of the Kwakwaka'wakw treasures began in 1973, as our people started to raise our voices together. The effort resulted in the creation of the U'mista Cultural Centre in Alert Bay in 1980, constructed in front of what was left of St Michael's Indian Residential School. The school was now closed and shuttered, and the Cultural Centre had been constructed to superimpose the view of the large brick edifice. Gloria Cranmer, the daughter of Chief Dan Cranmer, founded the centre to repatriate the masks and cultural objects that we had lost. She and her brother, Chief Bill Cranmer, worked tirelessly to bring life back into 'Yalis, to the Kwakwaka'wakw from all villages, to ask them to come home. I had helped Gloria in narrating a film to honour the opening of U'mista that year, and I had begun to attend other Potlatches.

Potlatches were more and more frequently practised in all of our traditional villages as we felt our way back into our culture. I would drop in and watch and listen at Potlatches, curious like everybody else. Soon, I started taking on the role of an official attendant, a role akin to a choreographer, escorting a dancer on the floor and guiding him or her as he held a large mask and moved to the rhythm. I was quickly elevated to speaker, narrating Potlatches for Elders who could not do it anymore.

One of the first things I learned about speaking at a Potlatch was that it is my role to call on the assembled to honour what they have witnessed, and to honour the healing memories in our culture. Everyone is a witness, and everyone is asked to walk with whomever is required to help and to inspire them along their way in life. If a speaker is good, the narrative creates meaning for all of the guests.

At one of these events, a matriarch from our village pulled me aside.

"Come here. Sit down," she said, conspiratorially. "I really dislike these gossipers. They're gossiping about you on the floor. You're an attendant at every Potlatch. Some of them, but not all of them, say you haven't earned your way into this process."

The matriarchs knew. The Kwakwaka'wakw knew. They were holding me to account. I was not perfect. I had only just started to attend Alcoholics Anonymous meetings. In the midst of my emergence from alcoholism, I would sit around with other alcoholics. We kept repeating our personal stories in a bid to find fellowship, to understand why we had made the choices we had. At the same time, I also immersed myself in books.

I felt as if admitting that I was reading self-help books sounded really desperate, but I knew that I'd better learn whatever I could from whatever source I could. I had discovered by this time that I had been a big enough fool to resist learning because of my history with residential school. Books helped me to develop an interest in other things besides pain and hurt. But I was still in a place of transition.

"So, you should get ready," the matriarch said to me, nodding, breaking through my wandering mind.

"What do you mean?" I asked, confused. I thought I was going to be told to stay away. I was just earning back my family's trust. I had to earn my place in the community.

"You have your own Potlatch. That'll keep them quiet."

I thought about it. I thought, "Okay, maybe she's right." If I really wanted to be helpful in the resurgence, the revitalization of my culture, I had to build true credibility.

I had to take a step out of the shadows.

———

MY FIRST Potlatch was at Gilford Island. I had come back home to where Granny had taught me the most important lessons of my life. Love is the foundation of everything. Love for the universe, for the world around us, for family, for self.

Everything was arranged really quickly. Potlatches can take years to put together, and I had everything done in a few weeks. I had lots of help. The Elders supported the idea; they were excited to see someone young inspired to take on this role, and they told me, and told my wife, that some of my speeches were wise.

People began to call me Nogad, wise.

Among the Kwakwaka'wakw People, once we exercise the right to host a P'asa, we may accept the honour of becoming a Chief. At the height of our existence, there were eighteen tribes, and every tribe had four or more clans, and each clan had its own ancestor. This means that each Kwakwaka'wakw clan is anchored by a Chief, called Hinumagame', a hereditary Chief. Usually it is the oldest sibling who garners this honour, but, in my case, my older brother passed before he could become a Chief after my father died.

There are different types of Chiefs as well, such as other standings called Dłaxwe' that entitle chieftainship, different from Hinumagame'. Over time, more chieftainships have evolved, and more Chiefs of varying histories and roles are among us. If you multiply those numbers, you may begin to see the number of Chiefs who can stand on a box of treasures.

Kwakwaka'wakw hereditary Chiefs lead our people's minds, hearts, and spirits, connecting us to everything that has come before us, and everything that was and is. When we open our box of treasures at the Potlatch, it is a time to give narrative to our history since the beginning. But more importantly, in revisiting this narrative, we are inviting all the offspring of that clan to belong, to be connected, to feel honoured to be a part of this family that can trace itself back to time immemorial. Young children, before residential schools, knew that they all belonged somewhere. They knew that we decided who the relatives were that belonged to this family.

Every time a Potlatch starts, I think that I am going to get tired of it, this rote narrative of our collective history, but that never happens. For this, my first Potlatch at Gilford Island, the Elders in their wisdom decided that my exercise would be to honour the narrative history of my wife's side of the family. Generally speaking, we recite the narrative history of our own paternal side. But in this case, my own Elders allowed me to see the beauty of the people I had chosen to live by my side— my wife's lineage, my children's lineage.

When I was little, I noticed that the Potlatch was a time for the Chiefs to make great speeches and to meet up with each other to talk. They would find a place in the forest, away from the rest of us, to make decisions about food sustainability, to negotiate economic and political tasks, to trade. But what I noticed as well was that the matriarchs were just as powerful. They wouldn't get up on the floor and speak, but their influence was felt in every decision that was made. Chiefs would return from their meetings to their wives to clarify terms of negotiation and then, resolved, would rejoin the men, something that has changed a little now that women are also recognized for their roles as Chiefs, but remains the same in its intention to involve everyone. The Potlatch was not only a time for honouring our past and celebrating our present, but also for planning for the future.

———————

I REMEMBER the last Potlatch I attended before I was an adult, when I was twelve and had returned to Kingcome Inlet for a short time. Ada had come storming out to the field where I was playing. I had lost interest and had wandered off.

"Come in quickly, your dance is coming up!" she called to me.

Chief Tom Patch Wamiss was the speaker and was an awesome figure resplendent in his regalia.

"Hurry up, go in the back of the curtain and be ready," he whispered to me.

But as I crossed behind the curtain, I was once again reminded of my separation from and embarrassment about who I was, and my feelings about being Indigenous. I always wanted to be a dancer, and most little boys like me wanted to be a Hamatsa, the wild cannibal dancer. I felt overwhelmed with anger, the rage filling me. I ran into the Big House, onto the dance floor, and yelled the wild scream of Baxwbakwalanuksiwe'. The problem was, that wasn't my dance. The singers, Chiefs, and Elders of the tribe all burst into laughter, and the Potlatch was delayed momentarily as everyone regained their posture. But at that moment, I rejected my culture, who I was, and that was the moment that began my true descent.

For me, the future had to be learning how to let go of this trauma. So much of trauma, and the anger that goes with it, goes unexpressed. It gets muddled up with drinking too much or overwork, or embodying too much emotional or physical control to settle the mind. And in all of this, at the heart of my emergence and my return to the Potlatch, I finally understood that human beings can help each other. Reaching out, being open, being honest, becoming accountable, and telling the truth. I didn't want to be angry anymore or hateful anymore or uncomfortable in my own body anymore.

For me, for so long, there was just no way to penetrate the wall of despair and hopelessness that, no matter what part of my life, I couldn't quite get past. Yes, I could do my work, and sometimes I would think I was very normal. But then I would capitulate to those memories of harm.

But there also were, and are, so many others like me.

There's something about being, or at least feeling, unloved. It's really hard to break. We have no skill set to emerge from that feeling. I started to notice that all of my beautiful grandparents, uncles, and aunts, they, too, didn't have that skill set. They couldn't arm me with ways to mitigate what had happened to me, or to them. Together, we knew only sadness and darkness and brokenness. Until I had my vision, every moment was a tense moment, where I would wonder if I was going to fall back into the dark again. That dark abyss, it was something that I had never found how to climb up out of, even when I had left the alcohol behind.

At that moment, looking out at everyone at my first Potlatch, I knew that I loved my family, my wife, and my children, all of my relatives. I loved them so much that I wanted them never to feel what I had felt.

And I could see all my relatives looking back at me.

The Potlatch—it had been beaten out of them. Their culture was denigrated in so many ways. I could not see that clearly for a long time. When the fog started lifting a little bit, I knew that my own redemption would have to include questioning what I was feeling by the time I was twelve, when I gave up on my culture, my knowing, myself.

The Indigenous residential school story has highlighted what really happened to us when we were colonized. Before the story exploded into the Canadian consciousness, returning to the Potlatch showed young people our resilience. Before we came together again and started talking about what was happening to us, and mourning our childhoods and remembering our strengths and our origins, none of us knew what on earth was happening to us.

Many years later, when I started to work with a working committee of the First Nations Summit, which eventually became the Indian Residential School Survivors Society, I began to attend more formal healing sessions. We Survivors would talk in circles about things that we thought we didn't know about ourselves, about what happened to us. As adult men and women, we discovered, in our malaise and fear, that we had experienced the same things as children. The first time we told these stories, we weren't hearing each other because the pain of discovery was too great. The next time, we started to piece together the similarities. After a period of time, I realized why we all suffered from the same afflictions, and it all began to make sense—our wounds were the same. The realization of how the word "trauma" applied to us was a revelation. Our individual stories together became a shared story, a fellowship, and we started to speak of our values, about finding out who we were, about allowing people to hear our stories, and reaching out to others who needed to tell their stories to the fellowship.

———

IN TIME, I DECIDED to have a Potlatch for Survivors. Everyone wanted to attend. In that two-day period, we handed out ninety traditional names for our children.

Everybody danced. We actually began to know each other a little bit more. I watched as our children began to become proud of their history again, and our ways. I tracked the difference between what I felt when we had to hide the Potlatch and what I could see, as an adult, happening among the children looking up at the dancers in my midst. The children all wanted to dance; they all wanted to recite their Genesis story. They wanted their true names.

We invited all of the Survivors at the gathering to come forward. Healing had to be, and is, a public matter. When people witness our stories and our healing, it means they not only witness that moment, but they're also forever going to inspire, encourage, and mentor those who need that healing. At the time, there was much that we did not know about those who needed to be healed, and about finding healers who could do the work. At the beginning, there was not much more than tears, the pain wresting us away from reaching out to each other. Our witnessing was more like a pronouncement than a process. But that Potlatch was the start of peeling the onion, the layers and obstacles to understanding. The shame that I felt since childhood had begun to lift, not only for me, but also for others.

We Survivors continued to meet in ceremony until the act of surviving eventually took on a different meaning.

Each of us learned that we have so much power when we're not afraid to use it.

Each of us learned that we can use our power in a good way.

Each of us learned that we are resilient, and we are open to healing.

And then came the healing circles, extending outward from the Indian Residential School Survivors Society, to the communities, to schools, to health care systems. We kept coming in, coming together; we kept telling our stories to each other. And that really clinched it for me: *telling each other our stories reveals, to us, the truth of letting go.*

Suddenly, I got it. I needed to hear those stories over and over and over again so that the light bulb could start to glow.

Over time, we can collectively elevate our consciousness, understanding, and willingness to heal from trauma. And once we get there, to that willingness, and we do begin to heal, we have to find ways to let it all go. We are closest to our highest selves when we empty the toxicity out of our lives and let go of the harm it causes us.

But we can only achieve this elevation of consciousness if we face it together—if we witness each other's pain and hear each other's stories.

I will say something perhaps controversial. For all of its hurtfulness, the Indigenous residential school story is a blessing in some ways. The Indigenous residential school story may be what will transform this country in galvanizing all of us, together. Canada will be a better country for knowing this story. Young Indigenous Peoples are regaining pride because they know this story. Survivors are heroes because they have told this story—the catalyst for all of us to pay attention.

To bring this blessing into fruition, however, we have to hold ourselves to a gold standard for consciousness in which the highest interest of the collective is what holds the line.

Our culture teaches us to remain in relationship with people. To hold the line, we have to break the silence and witness not only each other's pain, but also our joy, and our hopes. We have to invite in circles of healing wherever we are: in schools, in communities, in homes, in places of worship. When we understand each other, and want to witness each other's emergence, that's when things really begin to change.

(14)

REDEMPTION

I N 1998, I was working in Campbell River, and I heard that Jane Stewart, Minister of Indian Affairs and Northern Development, was going to make a speech on the occasion of the unveiling of Canada's Aboriginal Action Plan. The speech was a response to the Report of the Royal Commission on Aboriginal Peoples that had been assembled over the course of several years. The Commission had taken on some of the work of looking into residential schools, and I wanted to hear what she had to say, so I rushed home from the office to watch the speech.

I walked in, and I sat down, and I listened. I waited for Jane Stewart to flatly and clearly say, for the residential schools, we are sorry. But what she said, at first, was that "the Government of Canada today formally expresses to all Aboriginal people in Canada our profound regret."

Regret.

I was enraged, sitting there by myself, wanting to scream at her on the television, wanting her to hear my anger. Yes, the word "sorry" was used in the speech, eventually, but what the government officially offered was regret. And that regret was not even offered by the prime minister in an official capacity, but as a sideline, a ministerial duty that was barely covered in the newspapers. For Indian residential school Survivors, the statement was too little, too late. A comprehensive and just settlement, one that would include an apology from the head of state, had not taken place.

In the 1990s, I was not the only one who felt enraged. Indigenous Peoples were being positioned by the governments of Canada and the media as radical and combative. Starting with the Oka Crisis in 1990, where the Mohawk Peoples created a blockade over a land treaty challenge in the town of Oka, Quebec, a number of protests were to follow, the majority of which were met by strong resistance from the RCMP and provincial courts. It was not only a fight over sovereignty, but over the ability of the Indigenous communities to stand up and say their piece. The 1995 dispute over Indigenous land in Ipperwash Provincial Park, Ontario, resulted in the death of Dudley George from the Stoney Point Ojibway band.

Many thought that the Royal Commission on Aboriginal Peoples, emerging after these successive protests, was a pointless exercise to appease Indigenous communities. We knew that changes to the economic value of land and resources found in traditional First Nations territories were exacerbating the issue, and rights and sovereignty decisions were affecting legal wranglings over land treaties, rather than digging deep to address the true and substantive issues that were at the heart of the matter: racism, colonialism, fear, and violence.

But all of that mattered less to me than the lack of a true apology.

Later that same day, I got a call from the First Nations Summit; they asked me to participate in a residential school Survivor working group, and they needed me to come down to North Vancouver on the very next Saturday. Fired up from watching the Stewart speech, I attended the meeting, and I barely remember what I said. Everybody else was focused on history, impacts, legacy, and I needed to talk about reconciliation, about our healing, about the need for a true apology. The need for true justice for every Survivor telling their story.

I had only just returned to Campbell River when they called me to come back. They wanted me to meet with the Board of Directors of the Indian Residential School Survivors Society. When I arrived, the eventual Lieutenant Governor of British Columbia, Steven Point, who was then the Tribal Chair of the Stó:lō Nation, met me at the door.

"Stay here," he said. "You'll have to wait. I'm in a meeting right now and I'll come back and talk to you when I'm done."

I thought he'd be a few minutes, but I sat outside his door for nearly an hour when he finally opened the door again.

"Robert," he said as the door cracked open, "You're now the executive director of the Indian Residential School Survivors Society."

———

APOLOGIES ASIDE, our organization had to decide how to respond to the rising number of criminal court cases being filed by Survivors. With the recognition of their trauma, and our ongoing re-traumatization in prisons, on the Highway of Tears, in Oka, and in Ipperwash, our people had started going to court in great numbers.

We had to decide what we were going to do on a national basis. Our organization was based in British Columbia, but there were all kinds of communities of Survivors everywhere across the country. There were individuals, the national Assembly of First Nations, a few Survivor organizations, churches, governments, lawyers representing Survivors—so many layers of Survivors and perpetrators, all trying to have their voices heard.

The federal government had created an alternative dispute resolution process to try and stave off all of the lawsuits. It wasn't working on any level. I spoke at a meeting of Survivors about the need to put a billion dollars into a fund for the Aboriginal Healing Foundation. That foundation was absolutely pivotal in igniting the healing process across the country. Some of my friends started calling me Billion-Dollar Joe because of that speech, but Jane Stewart's ministry refused to add any more to the $350 million they had in place, suggesting that they didn't trust Indigenous Peoples to spend it wisely. On top of this, despite the framework in place, lawsuits were still going forward because very few people believed in the alternative dispute resolution process. The government blamed the churches, some of the churches blamed the government, teachers who were found guilty of abuse were also blaming the system, and as these legal cases were bandied about, Survivors were the ones losing out.

And Survivors were dying. The more years that passed, and the fewer of us that were left to tell our stories and to gain justice, the deeper objectives of our need for healing and acknowledgement.

In my role with the Indian Residential School Survivors Society, I became co-chair of the National Working Caucus on Residential Schools, eventually called the Truth-Sharing, Healing, and Reconciliation Roundtable. We heard that the settlement parties were negotiating: the federal government, Assembly of First Nations, churches, Survivors, and Survivor organizations. In fact, even in her abdication of an apology, Jane Stewart was able to support the establishment of the Aboriginal Healing Foundation, and Georges Erasmus, its president, had gone to the assembly of the United Church and set them a challenge to push for a national inquiry into residential schools. Among all of the churches responsible, the United Church took the lead on facilitating our collective work toward healing, so there was momentum to change the narrative in this direction. My cousin, Alberta Billy, was the first to demand an apology from her own United Church congregation, which was given and others followed suit. The United Church was ready to acknowledge what needed to be done.

As a country, we're always stuck in our own rules. How we advocate, and how we push things forward, should be better than what they are. But if you're not government, you're not going to win. Very rarely.

At our caucus sessions, therefore, we started with healing. It was something that we could advance, no matter what else was taking place. Our first and foremost goal in the process was to allow all parties involved in the residential school system to tell their stories, in public and in private. We wanted to provide validation for Survivors and others affected by the legacy of the schools, along with a public record.

At the same time, I was still working with changing the alternative dispute resolution process. In fact, at one point, we were arguing about the release of funds, and the government wanted an absolute guarantee that once we had agreed through the process, they would never be liable for any additional damages in the future. I was the chair of that meeting.

"I don't think we can go any further with the Indigenous Caucus of this committee," I said. "We need to go and sit down by ourselves. I don't think we can sign this, ever."

There were a lot of distasteful elements in the entire process. But there were still eighty thousand Survivors alive, and I wanted to make sure that they would benefit from all of this work. We needed to do something. If we dragged it out, pushed it too long, there would be nobody left to benefit. And yet there were still different factions at work. Phil Fontaine, as National Chief of the Assembly of First Nations, launched a class action lawsuit on behalf of the First Nations, Survivor, Deceased, and Family Class. It was settled out of court in 2006, which brough the $2 billion Indian Residential Schools Settlement Agreement into effect the next year. Each qualified person was to receive $10,000 for attending a school, plus $3,000 for each year at the school, plus additional compensation for abuse. We decided on a series of points as a way of mapping the conditions and effects of abuse, although some found it controversial. The system might not have been perfect, but it was a start—it was a recognition.

We kept working at it. And through all of our discussions, as best as we could, we kept returning to the fact that what Survivors needed most was to create a safe place to tell our stories, and a working space to get to the truth.

The more we talked about it, the more we realized that a public inquiry was not an option. We realized that it would not help because of the futility of getting an agreement from the prime minister at the time, and that we should promote the idea of a Truth and Reconciliation Commission. Everybody agreed. For the next year and a half, beginning just after Phil Fontaine started his suit, we explored the options. We drew in expertise and Indigenous experiences from South Africa, Australia, New Zealand, and Chile. We explored the nature of systemic harm. The nature of colonialism in practice. The underlying reason for the schools, and the destruction of the so-called Indian desired by the governing factions in Canada for hundreds of years. We kept pushing for holistic justice.

I think our work had its own life. None of us created it independently, but everything that we developed seemed to be a vehicle for Survivors.

———

I WENT THROUGH the settlement agreement process myself.

I worked with a lead assessor, a man named Rodger Linka—a good man from Saskatchewan. Rodger slowly, carefully, marked down everything that I told him: the sexual abuse, the beatings, the name-calling, bending over naked and strapped on a chair in front of all my friends, all of my relatives. He listened deeply.

My experiences, my abuse, my time, my body, my culture, my fear amounted to seventy-three points.

———

IN 2008, the Truth and Reconciliation Commission was to be announced in Ottawa on the floor of the House of Commons. Prime Minister Stephen Harper was going to offer an apology, one wholly unlike Jane Stewart's a decade earlier. But a few days before the actual day of apology, the prime minister invited four of us to sit with him: an Inuit male Elder, a Métis woman, a fiery young lady from the Manitoba Métis Federation, and me.

In the back of my head, looking at the prime minister, I thought, "This guy's playing it all wrong." It seemed like a setup, a means to cater to voters. And there was this really striking gentleman sitting off to one side, exuding power and authority, but saying nothing. He was never introduced to us, and I had assumed he was the prime minister's adviser. He may simply have been a page or security guard, but the whole time we were in that room I felt like we were being watched. It felt a bit strange that we never knew his name and yet he was there, watching us, listening.

When we started what began an afternoon-long discussion, I told the prime minister that I was going to speak last, because what I had to say was really important. All of my peers spoke well. They covered everything I wanted to cover. They spoke of what mattered to them, to their communities, to Survivors. I kept my silence. The prime minister listened to all three people and then looked at me.

"Well?" he said.

"Thank you," I said. "The reason why I wanted to speak last is because I wanted to say that Canadians need to know that we have to go through this thing called reconciliation. In your speech, after reciting the apology, you've got to end in a place of hope. You've got to invite people into a process of reconciliation."

I had no idea whether or not he was listening to me. There were handshakes and thank-yous, and we left his office. I was supposed to watch from the floor of the House of Commons with Chief Willie Blackwater, whose residential school legal case predated our changes to the alternative dispute resolution process, and was a precedent for much that we eventually incorporated into our beautifully flawed points system. But I went up to the balcony, where I thought I'd make less of an interruption as I was running late.

I couldn't see anything, but I could hear the prime minister's words as he started to speak.

I was holding my breath. We had just poured everything into our work: all of my people, all Survivors, all of my relatives were holding our breath waiting for this moment.

The apology was beautiful. I read it later. But I did not hear anything at all that day until I heard the words, "for this we are sorry."

My eyes flooded with tears, and I did not have to hear another word of that speech. I waited in the balcony long enough to clear my head a little bit, then got up and walked out of the House of Commons, ran across the field in front of Parliament Hill, and jumped into a cab. I went straight to the airport and flew home.

I had heard what I wanted to hear.

Later, I found out that former Prime Minister Stephen Harper had changed his speech. He had listened. In his 2008 "Statement of Apology to Former Students of Indian Residential Schools," the last words he said were:

A cornerstone of the Settlement Agreement is the Indian Residential Schools Truth and Reconciliation Commission. This Commission presents a unique opportunity to educate all Canadians on the Indian Residential Schools system. It will be a positive step in forging a new relationship between Aboriginal peoples and other Canadians, a relationship based on the knowledge of our shared history, a respect for each other and a desire to move forward together with a renewed understanding that strong families, strong communities and vibrant cultures and traditions will contribute to a stronger Canada for all of us.

A STRONGER CANADA for all of us is not simply about reconciling with Indigenous histories. A stronger Canada for all of us requires openness, as well as truth.

Throughout the Truth and Reconciliation Commission process I travelled the country, speaking to Survivors. These others, like me but each having their own story, changed me. These Survivors changed the playing field for reconciliation because of their courage and their bravery and their willingness to share their pain. Their experiences. Their spirits. They did the beautiful thing—the thing that may be able to allow us to rebuild this entire country and make it better.

When I look at Canada, and the newcomers coming here from everywhere on Earth, all of the races, all of the religions—they all have a story to tell. We like to applaud ourselves for being open to these newcomers despite the wall we have created of wrongful assumptions, prejudice, and racism. This wall exists because we have lost sight that everybody has a story. When the first wave of newcomers came to our shores, they attempted to assimilate us by destroying our languages and cultures. Thus, we have a caution to make to our newcomers coming to our traditional homelands: Be true to yourselves. Do not lose your souls in assimilation in the name of "being Canadian." Bring your foreign languages and your ancient rituals and practices with you. As Indigenous Peoples we welcome you here. We are neither frightened nor challenged by your diversity and resourcefulness. And yet, your diversity strains to be acknowledged and respected in Canada. Many are not open to hearing these stories. Many are not open to facing our own discomfort.

And it's so simple an idea, but one that, hopefully, everyone will understand.

Each of us has to face ourselves and determine how we will respond to the legacy of the residential schools. Determine where our pain lies in our own life story. Each of us has to start listening to the stories around us, and seek out those stories, as well.

Here's why.

All of the people who come to Canada have different rituals and traditions. We must bring all of these together to make a container for knowledge that works for everybody. When we pour into that container from each other's cultures, without judgment or criticism, we may be able to create an even better, shared culture.

When we are all one, we benefit from what serves us best. What serves us all.

The spirit of reconciliation is one that builds core values that we have to exercise daily so that they become second nature to us. We have to begin to know that we're not *just us* alone. We have to begin to know that we are not just responsible for ourselves, but to everybody else. We have to begin to know that we have to stop the politicization of our responses and become human beings in our ability to listen and learn from each other.

We're slowly shifting our mindset. That was unthinkable a few years ago. Five, six years down the road what we are doing will also be unthinkable, because we've broken some more barriers. It really is that journey of a thousand steps. I do not want to discourage you. In my cultural tradition, we say it will take seven generations to achieve a change. Our first step has already been a success.

But we have to do what we can do right now. We cannot wait for the holy grail, or a magic wand, to begin to listen to each other.

Reconciliation has to start with self. Period.

Every moment I get a little better than I was in the last moment. I am healing. And I, for one, do not want to wait seven generations or longer.

(15)

WORKING TOWARD PERFECTION

—————

DON'T EVER have acrimonious meetings in hot summer weather.

In Ottawa, even after we started the process of launching the Truth and Reconciliation Commission, all the leaders of the mainstream organizations were still coming together to do the work. There were still some really angry Survivors. That made sense.

But then there were the church people.

The $2 billion Indian Residential Schools Settlement Agreement of 2006 had determined that the Catholic, Anglican, United, and Presbyterian churches all contribute to the overarching fund and reparations. The United Church led the way, and the Anglican and Presbyterian churches quickly followed suit. But there was an outlier.

Millions of dollars that were intended for residential school Survivors were spent on Roman Catholic Church lawyers, administration, a private fundraising company, and unapproved loans. The Catholic Church—the largest and most influential of all the churches involved in the residential school system, and in fact the church that had lobbied for the system in the first place—reneged on its legal requirements. The $29 million in cash that was supposed to be paid by 2012 at the latest, according to the Supreme Court, was absorbed back into church budgets. A fundraising goal of $25 million on top of this never took place, as the church was supposed to ask its members to give of themselves to this effort and simply did not. Serious accounting discrepancies brought to light in 2012 were never justified, including over a million dollars spent on creating a shell corporation to manage funds that were supposed to be paid to Survivors. This is a matter that, as I write these words, is still being played out in the courts.

And now, it was Ottawa in summer. It was hot, and I was upset. Apparently after all these months, these years of healing, now I jumped back to a point of pure frustration.

There was a break for lunch, and I decided to take a walk instead. I was despondent. I came to an intersection, and I saw this big church on the opposite side of the street. I looked at the church and ran through the traffic. Inside the doors, I fell onto my knees and I prayed.

Out loud, I started asking questions.

"God, are you here? Are you with us? Allow me the energy to go back to the meeting and pick up the pieces. It doesn't matter what the end result is."

I kept hearing the Christians tell me that God is a really forgiving deity. If I didn't quite understand it, given my experience with the negotiations with the Truth and Reconciliation Commission and the churches, that was okay. Kneeling in that church, I felt a connection to the universe again, and I knew that everything was going to be okay. I knew that everything that I was feeling was part of this process, and that I just had to work my way through it.

We at the Voluntary Truth and Reconciliation Commission Roundtable created space for exploring the human condition at the heart of reconciliation, wanting something bigger, better, and forward looking. But what mattered was trust, good faith, vulnerability, and the value of an ancient imperative of working toward perfection.

———

THE ANGLICAN Church Senate on Vancouver Island had invited me to be their guest speaker. This was a time when, in the Cariboo Region in the interior of British Columbia, one of their churches had been sued by Survivors so heavily that they were under threat of being able to maintain their congregation. They were losing their premises; the building and their land was being repossessed.

I didn't know what I was going to say. I hadn't really thought about it, perhaps because I wasn't quite sure why I was there. The whole church was feeling sorry for itself. When I was called up to speak, I knew what I had to say.

"This is really, really simple," I said, "Come on, get your chins off the floor. Why are you moping? What, you've lost your building? So what? You *are* the church. You need *people* here more than you need a building."

"We love these monuments," someone piped in. "They're beautiful and sacred."

"Without these buildings, you'd still be here, and you have to start by doing what you've always done. Care for the poor. Advocate for justice. Love people. You can still do that with or without all of your glorious buildings."

I was thinking about the building, and I agreed that they can be sacred. The images that we see of churches can represent certain things in our minds, and the biggest of them all is love.

If we ever truly are reconciled, then we will still need churches, but we may not need religion. It won't matter, on any given Sunday, or any day, what church we go to. They do have an important place in our lives, but that importance is not tied to a catechism, a set of rules.

The world is better, I do not know how much, because of the way that churches can lead in a community, not how many rules they put into place.

The challenges occur in religions when they cause division between people. When religions create situations where we never get the full experience of knowing each other, and therefore the distance between us gets bigger than we can handle. Those are the times when, at that moment the chasm grows too large; we stop understanding, and we start becoming afraid. We hate what we are scared of, and the process becomes cyclical: When we are scared, we do not allow people to really get to know us. We become guarded, perhaps not in all parts of our lives, but in most.

The reason that the residential school system existed is because of this fear.

On April 12, 1876, the Indian Act was introduced to deliberately eradicate First Nations' cultures in favour of assimilation with colonizers. It meant that Indigenous men had to voluntarily give up their own rights to treatied land if they wanted to vote federally, and women were not allowed to vote at all, even within the new band system. Prime Minister John A. Macdonald authorized the creation of the residential school system so that the government might isolate Indigenous children from their families and cut all ties to their cultures.

But why? These decisions were not put into place because European cultures were better. That simply wasn't true. There was nothing wrong with the paradise we had created here already. These decisions happened because colonizers were afraid that they were not really in control, that they might lose the little control they had over the vast land and the hundreds of nations surrounding their tiny cities. These decisions happened because colonizers were afraid that they would lose access to a rich and generous land. Perhaps there were other fears as well.

Residential schools operated as early as 1831, the first being the Mohawk Institute in Brantford, Ontario. While these schools were institutional, they were also experimental. Most of them were run by Jesuit missionaries, connected to churches established before Canada became a dominion. The first federal, custodial residential schools were introduced in 1883—three prairie schools. By 1930, there were eighty, and by the time they were closed in 1996, there had been more than 130 of these schools assimilating, abusing, isolating, and hurting little children across the country.

In 1904, Dr Peter Bryce was hired by the government of Canada to be their Chief Medical Officer, studying the health of the children in their care. By that year, reports were already coming in that half of the children in the care of the churches and the state were dying. Dr Bryce did not blame the situation on Indigenous children's bodies or their parents' culture. He blamed the government and the government's negligence of these children. He even reported that Indigenous children left at home with their families were robust and healthy—healthier than even colonists' babies, with higher birth weights and happy faces. Dr Bryce loved his work, and he advocated for justice, spending over two decades working to try to raise awareness. He had the full experience of knowing Indigenous Peoples, and he knew that nothing in their lives needed to be controlled. Even when he was shut down by the federal government who had hired him, he never stopped trying to end the residential school system.

What has happened in churches, and in governments, is that they would not admit to their failure. Each of these controlling bodies had their own interests to protect, which led to acts of desperation. None of their efforts prior to the creation of the residential schools had succeeded in quelling Indigenous Peoples' strengths. It was only through the death of their children that Indigenous communities began to fall apart, as it would have been for English and French families had they ever been compelled to the same fate.

All in all, most colonial impositions on the world really haven't worked out well.

In reconciliation, we have all finally admitted to our failures. The opposite of fear is called honesty. And it's called trust. And it's called openness.

We have nothing to fear from the truth. When everybody gets to know each other, there is no fear. You are your best and you are your worst—at all times. You are your vulnerabilities, your strength, and your resilience, all at once. Everything about you can be revealed, and everything will be fine. Knowing that really breaks down walls, right? You have nothing to fear from me. I have nothing to fear from you. Because when I've told you all I can, and I've even told you what I felt uncomfortable to tell you, then there is nothing left to hide.

All of these virtues begin to shift the experience of human relationships. Whether these truths emerge from vision, or from a dialogue circle, or sharing a workspace, or friends going to the movies together, they allow for an appreciation of who we really are.

———

I ATTENDED A World Council of Indigenous Peoples event in Jerusalem.

As a child who went to Christian residential schools for a long time, I was really confused about Christianity, about how Christian churches orchestrated the utter waste of my own people. And yet, I believe in God, or, at the very least, believe in the Creator I have known since my birth.

Yet, in travelling with the council through Palestine, we were moving alongside a river trying to find a place to get through with all of our vehicles. I asked a friend of mine what river we were passing. Someone told me that it was the River Jordan. It's not a big river. There's a backpool of water that amounts to no more than a trickle.

"Oh my gosh," I said. "This is where John the Baptist baptized Jesus. I'm not going by this place without getting baptized."

One of our crew was a priest, and someone asked him to baptize me. The whole caravan stopped. There was even a hut at the side of the river where there were gowns for sale for people to be baptized in. I have a picture of myself being submerged into that trickle of water, and we ended the day at the Sea of Galilee.

Despite my exposure to Christianity and the stories of Jesus through residential school, I was just mesmerized by the experience. And I sat there and realized that the events of the day just added further to my confusion.

Where does the truth lie? What I know is that I have a modern respect for Jesus. There is no question he was a good man and spiritual in his way. When I think about all the different visions we have of a God, and so many great men and women who don't agree with each other, I recognize that we can remember to do what we've always done. Care for the poor. Advocate for justice. Love people.

No matter what spiritual tradition we follow, we are always following the same path. We are seeking and we are finding that elusive inner self—the self that wants to be connected, that wants to be known, and that wants to be loved.

We have nothing to fear.

(16)

OUT OF THE WILDERNESS

OST OF us are afraid of our shadows.

There was no dance at the Potlatch more commanding than the Hamatsa, once performed by a young boy, an honour now shared with both young men and women in our present day. The initiate to the Hamatsa society would exile into the woods for an extended period of time to become possessed by the cannibal spirit at the North End of the World, Baxwbakwalanuksiwe'. The intent of this ceremony was simply for the boy to become untethered to other humans, to learn about his own survival. And to learn, even more importantly, about himself.

What were his deepest fears?

What were his failures?

What was important to him?

My friend Ernie became a Hamatsa at G̲wa'yas-da̲m's when he was little. Ernie is remembered as the last Hamatsa who was exiled into the woods for an extended time, four days and four nights, but he found out later that he was never alone or by himself. An adult was always nearby in observance, always concealed. The ancient custom demanded that he come face-to-face with himself; he had to confront his deepest fears. He had to learn to become one with the elements. He would have to become the ultimate survivalist. He learned many things that would be guideposts for his life's journey.

Ernie and I were about the same age. I watched as the Chiefs, singers, and healers proceeded to the edge of the forest behind the Big House to greet him, and to escort him back into the Hamatsa society and the community at large. But, possessed by the cannibal spirit, the Hamatsa was driven into a temporary and symbolic insanity. Ernie had learned how to fend for himself in the wilderness, and the Elders needed to receive and transform the new Hamatsa initiate back from this state of insanity to normalcy.

Ernie's shriek of "Hap! Hap!" that terrifying cry of a wild man, could be heard as he approached. When he appeared at the edge of the forest, clothed in only hemlock boughs, the Kumya ceremony began so that his attendants, those who had been initiated themselves, could corral and guide him carefully with the sound of rattles, chants, and songs. Ernie was guided to the front entrance of the ceremonial house where he bolted in, still shrieking. He circum-navigated the floor in a clockwise direction, guided by attendants, and then disappeared behind a curtain that served as a thin veil between the worldly and the supernatural.

When calm was restored, the initiate yelled again from behind the curtain. Attendants quickly restrained his movement and escorted him around the dance floor. No one was harmed or bitten by the cannibal spirit. Attendants, who were all Hamatsa themselves, concealed him while four Chiefs were summoned to bring sacred objects of cedar in which to dress him. Once again, we heard the terrifying shriek of Baxwbak-walanuksiwe' and the attendants stepped away to let the initiate dance. At first, Ernie danced with a slight frenzy, still being possessed. After the fourth song he began to be more measured, more composed. He yelled once more and sprang into a gut-yelling "Hap! Hap!" as the attendants escorted him through the veil.

Absolute silence prevailed, followed by the cacoph-ony of wood beaks clapping. These bird monsters were the attendants of Baxwbakwalanuksiwe'. There was Huxhux, the bird with a long beak, followed by Galukwame, the Crooked Beak of Heaven; G̲wax̲gwak-walanuxiwe', the Raven of the North End of the World; and Hamasiwala, the face of Baxwbakwalanuksiwe' himself. When the bird monsters had exited, the new initiate came out one more time to circumnavigate the fire and vanish behind the sacred screen. The final act included the Hiligexte leading the new Hamatsa in a final dance of celebration while the Elder Hamatsas danced in support and honour. Every eye would be glued to the new member of the Hamatsa in his regalia, powerful and graceful in motion. Hiligexte had succeeded again through her healing powers to restore the Hamatsa to the family.

During this time, there were similar rituals for young girls, rituals with which I am less familiar, but that served the same purpose: to understand themselves and their relationship to the world around them, and to enter back into the community with an awakened knowledge.

———

I NEVER received this initiation, taken, as I was, into the confines of St Michael's Indian Residential School at such a young age.

But I remember. I remember watching Ernie take off the hemlock boughs of the wilderness and emerge in sacred cedar attire, changing over into the regalia of someone who was welcomed into the fold, who was beginning to discover his strengths, transforming from the wild boy he was into a quieted young man. Finally, the Hamatsa would be adorned in a beautiful costume representing his clan—a Thunderbird, a raven, an orca—and he would be celebrated and dance around by himself for the first time.

As you can imagine, going into the wilderness at a very young age, even at five or six years old, or maybe a little older, most of us would be afraid of our shadows. You truly are backed up against your fears. You can't run, can't hide—you're in it. And so your fears become real. In a place like that, you have to face your fears and actually live through those moments of terror.

Imagine what you might have learned about yourself in such a ritual. When you are young, you might not be able to put those teachings into words, but the teachings are courage, resilience, endurance. At the same time, youth going through this training would learn to relate to all the wilderness and its elements: how to live with squirrels, bears, and snakes, and understand the lives of these animals. You learn that you are part of something. Even the darkness and the fear elevate your mind. You begin to wonder about the universe, and everything about the world around you that you weren't familiar with before.

As I had never experienced this ritual, this healing, this preparation for the life ahead of me—as I had been deliberately and fearfully distanced from my clan, my family, my home—I had to find my way out of the wilderness by myself. By the time I was twelve, as you may recall, I was both begging to become a Hamatsa and embarrassed by the ritual.

For me, what has allowed me to find my way, and to heal, is that I remembered the magic. I remembered seeing the universe open up to me through the eyes of the dancers behind their beautiful masks. I remembered who I was, as a Kwakwaka'wakw man. But I did not know myself, my strength, and how to find my way back home until I truly learned how to love myself. In the work that I have done on finding my way, I know that there is always something that continues to surface. There is always some trigger that will challenge me, for better or for worse, but it is a process of coming back to myself, coming back to remembering who I am and that I belong. And all of the residential school Survivors have had to find their way out of that wilderness in their own ways.

———

WHEN I think about all of the people who contributed to the early stages of reconciliation, our first meetings between politicians and Survivors, it was really nasty. We had seven national dialogues that took place to begin to unwrap all of the issues. There were some basic moral, ethical, overarching principles that had brought us to this point: Nobody leaves the circle, no matter how uncomfortable or angry they are. We had a big problem, and we had to figure out how to resolve it.

Over the course of this work, we heard from more than seven hundred witnesses just as the Truth and Reconciliation Commission engaged its own witnesses and collectively assessed the more than five million records provided by the government, creating a historical record of the residential school system, and worked to engage the Canadian public to educate people about the history and legacy of the residential school system.

As I observed and watched over our own seven national dialogues, the meaning and impact of real dialogue became clear. The first dialogue was the most acrimonious of course. The next one was a little gentler, the third one there were tears. By the time we arrived at the fourth dialogue, there was some forgiveness. It was not until the fifth one that we were able to understand that we could work together, that the government would begin to honour our stories. And that was a huge step. Nobody talks about this; nobody, perhaps, even looks back and realizes that, had we not gone through all of those dialogues, we probably wouldn't have gotten as far as we did.

In June 2015 in Ottawa, the Truth and Reconciliation Commission presented its summary report, including 94 Calls to Action to further the reconciliation process.

These calls to action are important. They are starting to be addressed, one by one. These very practical pillars are what we need to create a plan, to put change in motion, and to address urgent needs such as the provision of basic rights and freedoms. Reconciliation won't happen without them. The infrastructure that the Truth and Reconciliation Commission creates is absolutely critical. We need to build monuments to change. We must address issues like water advisories. We can provide our younger generations with political training. We need to spend time raising the quality of life for ordinary mothers and girls, as well as their nieces and nephews.

But the calls to action are not all that reconciliation is. Reconciliation is more than this.

If we are only looking at our reckoning of material things, our balancing of rights and wrongs, when it's all said and done, we're still behaving badly with and about each other. Focusing on the calls to action alone precludes us from reviewing and examining reconciliation in all of its depth, and breadth, of its potential. Reconciliation requires us to see ourselves and where we have set our goals, and why we have created those goals. On a personal level, reconciliation, for me, always comes back to love.

We all need to be reconciled to love.

And yet there are many of the unreconciled among us.

Everything is incremental. There's no home run in this reconciliation idea. Every little step we take is reconciliation. Reconciliation is not what happens when cameras are on us, when the radio is broadcasting every word. One of my concerns about reconciliation in general in Canada is that most of our attention is on political reconciliation.

Reconciliation happens when nobody's there except us.

Reconciliation happens where we live and work. Reconciliation happens in what people do to recover from the past. Reconciliation happens from the ground up, the real ground, where we are able to knock on each other's door, to stop each other on the playground, and say hello. I suspect that this is true for changing the world in any capacity.

In all of the work that I have done, I have found that we still haven't really found a way to be comfortable with each other. Those who have and those who do not have. Those who are well and those who are not. What we need is to bridge the gap and have a discussion, a really good discussion about who we are, and what matters to us.

In 2012, I convened a council of Elders from Vancouver to gather at the unceded territories of the Musqueam Nation, Knowledge Keepers of the histories and of the cultures that they came from. I wanted to sit with them for a day or two, to talk about the kind of work we were engaged in, and to seek advice and direction and support from the moral and spiritual Elders of different traditions: There were representatives from Judaism, Chinese Buddhism, Islam, Elders from South Asia, Indigenous Peoples, and more. And it proved to be a really wise step. Reconciliation includes everybody, and Elders from all of the different traditions were more than willing to sit in a circle for two days to talk about what it meant.

Our main question was this: In your ancient cultures, how did you practice reconciliation? Is there a word in your language for this? I really wanted to know if all of these Elders had a definition for what reconciliation was to their traditions, and whether reconciliation was an ancient imperative. I believed that if that was the case, it would be an easier proposition to pass this message on to young people. There was no question that all of their ancient traditions had a concept or understanding of reconciliation. What was really exciting, along with that discovery, was that all of these Elders believed that reconciliation was a noble idea, part of a process that calls people together to figure out who they are, as individuals and as collectives, to talk about these matters openly and in safe ways. They were all committed.

INDIGENOUS LANGUAGE is a language of the land. Everything—the people, the animals, the fish, the birds that fly at the shoreline—is so interconnected, interweaving, that our words are connected to the oneness of everybody, every thing.

To emerge from the wilderness, we must accept this oneness.

We must teach our children love before anything else; life is not just about finding material success. We all must remember, deeply, who we are. And we must continue to talk with one another. If reconciliation is going to sustain itself, it will also always have to exist with a heavy emphasis on the next generation behind us. We need our children to understand reconciliation, to practise it, to embrace it. We need our children to remember who they are—to deeply, deeply remember.

I remember who I am. And I'm not such a bad person.

It's like love. If you never talked about love at length, how are you going to know what it is? We need to ask these questions. How can we work together, and live side by side? How can we create love and mutual respect and inspiration?

Reconciliation should be a virtue, a core value, and it should suffuse the way that we live and breathe. We need to start by thinking about our own lives and what needs reconciling. It could be a broken relationship, or it could be family squabbles, or it could be substance abuse, or fear. That's what everybody ignores: What can we do with our own lives to become aware of where the damage is done? If you're open to change and transformation, and willing to look beyond your despair and not remain a victim, that's the basis for hope. And in doing so, you begin to engage, and you start to unravel all of the complications in your life. And it is our duty to pass on what we have learned along the way about what is right, even if we have lived miserable lives. Everything is a lesson: every experience of joy, grief, despair, and brokenness. But every one of these experiences is also a chance for us to come together.

To emerge from the wilderness, we must be committed to reconciliation on every level of our lived experience.

When we are committed, and when we are intentional in being reconciled individually, collectively this will change this whole damn world.

(17)

THE RELEASE

TANDING AT the top of the steps of St Michael's Indian Residential School, one final time in 2015, I spoke before the brick building came crashing down.

There was no redeeming grace about taking little children away from their families, homes, and communities; destroying their sense of pride and their language; and stripping them of the ability to have loving relationships with their parents and family. The theme of this gathering was to mark the passing of a dark era and look to the future with hope and optimism. We cannot be defined by that building and that history. If we define ourselves that way, we will be doomed to pass on the same characteristics of pain, of fear, and of hunger to the next generation.

I felt the energy of the people around me, together for the same purpose: to heal. You could feel the energy and the joy and the hope in the murmurs in the crowd and the momentum leading up to that day, to reconciliation, to ending some small part of our collective grief.

There, I also had an absolute moment of just me. I thought back about how I had come a long way from that other time when I stood at the top of the stairs, never looking back, looking out at the emptiness in front of me.

Both times, I was elevated. Once, in 1958, I was elevated with the relief of shutting that door behind me but knowing on some level that St Michael's would not leave me, not then, and perhaps not ever. I was elevated with the exhilaration of knowing that there was an ending, and a beginning.

But now, I was here with others. All of these people. And as I looked out around me, I thought: it's possible. There's reason to believe. There's reason to hope.

I didn't know for sure before then. Everything I'd done in my work and my journey to reconciliation had started from zero. I always believed that I really had a lot to learn if I was going to move this forward. So I did; I built little blocks on which to step. To move reconciliation forward. To move myself forward. All I ever knew for sure, at each moment, was that I had to take one step at a time, whether it was a step away from despair and hopelessness, or whether it was standing before this throng of people.

Anticipating reconciliation is a really high bar to think about for all of society. But that's how powerful and impactful that moment was for me, as I looked out in front of me and with each step I took.

Six years later, in 2021, the first ever National Day for Truth and Reconciliation, in tandem with Orange Shirt Day, I returned to Alert Bay and to the former grounds of St Michael's Indian Residential School once again, under a darkened sky. With no time to spare after a television interview, I dashed down to the marshalling grounds for the planned walk to the site and tried hard to be inconspicuous, melding into the crowd of orange-clad marchers. I was still trying to catch my breath when I was called to the front of the sea of orange before me and asked to make opening remarks and to say a prayer to start the march.

I walked to the front of the throng and turned to face the people.

It's funny standing in front a lot of people. For some reason or another, these people, both Survivors and many others, had heard about reconciliation. For some reason or another, they wanted to hear what I was going to say. And I was thinking, "I'm just little old me. I'm near the end. And I've been through hell and back. And I'm here, just lucky to be here with you."

I was fixated by the little children holding up a huge banner that covered the width of Front Street. They seemed so small, like we once were at St Michael's

Indian Residential School. Bewilderment filled their faces to fully comprehend why they were there, just like we might have been as little children when we couldn't understand where we were going and why.

It was in that moment that I experienced heart stutters and shook with a deep, internal cry with no tears.

I was in the right place. I wanted to be with people who had attended St Michael's Indian Residential School. These were the people who experienced the indecency, loss, and harm that I had gone through. I wanted to stand with them and to tell them that this was a new time of hope and promise. I wanted to applaud them for their courage and resilience; to show that they mattered and had worth.

The significance of the marshalling grounds seared into my memory through a flashback. In my first year at St Michael's Indian Residential School, I remember a gate owned by BC Packers Fishing Company that divided the Indian and white ends of town at night. I know that racism was present, daily, at the many canneries along the coast. Indians, Chinese, Japanese, and whites were always segregated by house arrangements and by wharf work sites. As I gazed at and spoke to the gathered crowd for the walk, I noticed that all of the Islanders were represented. Cormorant Island has for some time now made efforts at collaboration.

As we walked up to the former school site, I noticed the Anglican Christ Church and its beautiful white picket fence, Cook's General Store, and the former homes of kind Elders who had once shared their tea and biscuits with us as children. As the crowd ringed the former site of the residential school building, we saw the orange plywood pyramid structure decorated with huge Thunderbirds and the slogan Every Child Matters, a temporary placeholder for what will be a permanent monument.

'Namgis Chief Don Svanvik welcomed all in attendance, applauding the Survivors at the gathering for their strength and resilience, encouraging them to continue their journeys of healing. I was flanked by two special people who were also former students of St Michael's: Chief Richard Dawson, who was a grandson of the great Chief Tom Dawson, on my left, and Pauline Alfred on my right, both fluent Kwak'wala language speakers.

On this date, we forever recommitted ourselves to the grand notion of reconciliation and asked the community to join us.

After listening to one of the great and sacred mourning songs handed down from the ancestors, a gentle and rhythmic beat that captured the spirit of the moment, we made our way to the Big House. A crackling fire welcomed us while the crowd settled in silent appreciation. It was good to be gathered in this safe and sacred place, and, at the last minute, I was asked to be the Big House speaker for the day, an honour and privilege.

I rose to my feet and called for everyone's attention, and for the singers to take their places at the log located at the front of our great house.

"Come, all of you. Come and take your places where you belong. Come and sing the mighty cry-songs that have been passed down to you from the ancestors. Come and complete the mourning ceremony that was started at the foreshore."

Ten women moved past a curtain meant to signify the thin veil between the natural world and the supernatural, between the mortal world and the spirit world. Wrapped in brilliantly coloured and designed ceremonial blankets, they filed to the front of the Big House floor and sat in seats facing the audience, heads slightly bowed and eyes downcast to create a stillness and quiet so hypnotic as to evoke the deepest human instinct to grieve.

When silence prevailed, I rose again to instruct the wise and knowledgeable singers to proceed with the mourning songs.

"Search and choose among our great mourning songs and let it be. We and our departed loved ones will all be free and at peace."

Three songs were sung at the Big House to complete the minimum four required, including the song we had heard at the school site. As the fourth song rose up to the roof of the Big House, the ladies, representing deceased loved ones, all stood and swayed in unison with arm and hand movements signifying the moment to move forward. This was the time to release loved ones into their eternal resting places.

With the mourning ceremonies completed, we were also able to rest and I called upon my precious relative Pauline to bless the feast.

While sitting quietly waiting to be served, I remembered a speech often made by Chief Tom Patch Wamiss at our gravesides.

> Go now!
> You have earned your rest!
> Go straight!
> Do not look back!
> You have decided to leave
> Go and be with the ancestors
> In time, we will all meet again
> Go now.

With the serving tables set, we dined together. We enjoyed steamed and barbecued salmon, fried and smoked eulachons, crab, shrimp, halibut, clam fritters, herring eggs, and eulachon grease.

While feast songs were sung tribe by tribe, the pain of Survivors' suffering and loss was set aside. Little boys danced the most coveted dance—the Hamatsa. Girls danced and swayed in majestic unison, blessing the floor, house, and everyone in attendance. The power of culture and the Big House was truly healing.

BUT THE DAY was not yet over. Under a shadowy nightfall, I travelled with Chief Gibby Jacobs from the Squamish Nation, and others, to Echo Bay and spent a night in the K̲'waxwalawadi Marina & Lodge preparing for what was to come.

The next day, I went home.

At G̲wa'yasdam̲'s, the next morning, I stepped onto the clamshell midden where I had spent most of my childhood before my arrival at St Michael's, a little paradise filled with everlasting good memories. I pointed out to Chief Gibby Jacobs the very site that our little oceanside one-room shack protruded over the water at high tide.

Making our way to the Big House located just behind our beach home, we found a roaring fire set for our small party, as Elder Chief Charlie Williams welcomed us all and people joined us from the village. Storytelling emerged in that space without instruction, and people in the chairs spoke of their knowledge, their history, culture, and village. The villagers were not only welcoming, but they were generous, serving a delicious and warm lunch with clam chowder and bannock and even homemade cinnamon buns.

We expressed our gratitude for this splendid reception before heading off to Hada, or Bond Sound. The trip didn't seem long at all as we glided past the scenic splendour of the Kwikwasut'inuxw Territory, greeted by dolphins and porpoises, a humpback whale, the great sea lions on the shore, and otters frolicking in our wake.

Hada is an ancient and timeless site where a contemporary dream and vision is literally unfolding before our eyes. The vision belongs to one of our young hereditary Chiefs, K'odi Nelson. What makes the vision all the more breathtaking and spectacular is that the place is the sacred site where Tsekame (the great cedar tree) transformed into the first ancestor of the Kwikwasut'inuxw Tribe. The very Genesis of our people, right here. Chief K'odi Nelson wants to invite the world to this sacred area to experience the natural powers of untouched wilderness and to learn the deep and mysterious culture of the original inhabitants, including a language and culture camp for Kwakwaka'wakw People and their children. It is a place where culture will become alive again and be the only place on Earth where Kwak'wala will be spoken in complete fluency.

Young people will learn to live off the land. It will be their place of spiritual sanctuary.

This place will contribute much to the healing and reconciliation that needs to be done.

It was there in my sacred land that I found myself back in our parallel universe, full of magic, full of imagination.

It was there in our culture's embrace that I found myself back in front of an always-sparkling open fire holding back the darkness, people dancing counter-clockwise around the light.

There were bears, wolves, and others from the forest kingdom. Those who belonged to the undersea world graced us with their presence, along with those that came from celestial places, entities that flew. The ghostly appearances of those from the spirit world enchanted us. It was sometimes scary and haunting, but it was captivating to see the animals, birds, aquatic creatures, ghosts, and spirits right in front of me.

I could reach out and almost touch them then.

I can reach out and touch them again.

(18)

FROM GENESIS
TO GENESIS

S TORYTELLING IS our way of life.

Our Genesis stories place us on our Awi'nakoła, our territories from time beginning.

These stories are deeply embedded in our language. In my own language of Kwak'wala, there are words like Gilga'lis, meaning "first one here." Nuyimagiwe' means "lead ancestor." Nuyimbalis is "a story throughout time and forever."

These are old stories, old words. The oldest carbon date of all our nations' presence on the coast of British Columbia, for example, places the Heiltsuk First Nation on their territories stretching back fifteen thousand years. In the earliest of times, these stories were told at Potlatches, but also in the home, or at work, and in smokehouses.

In my own Kwakwaka'wakw history, these entities are intertwined through their origin stories as well as their enjoining territories for political, social, economic, cultural, and spiritual reasons. They have sustained their allegiance to each other, and together, we have shaped each other's worldviews.

Our clearly delineated territories created a sense of membership within each clan that reinforced the meaning of belonging. Being meticulous about Genesis narratives created the very pillars of our evolution. These stories predicated and formed our spiritual practices. From out of all these stories came our government structures, laws, concepts of sharing wealth. The Potlatch emerged as an overarching constitutional framework to live by in the community. Ceremonial houses, our Big Houses, became the temples where space was held for Chiefs to validate their perspectives with those who listened. Each displayed their boxes of treasures, which upheld their honour and place and which, metaphorically, contained all of their rights, dances, songs, names, coppers, histories, and everything else of significance. Family laws, marriages, and adoptions were ritualized in the Potlatch. Rites of passage were performed. Coming of age rituals for girls were honoured. Births and deaths were marked. Names and dances were placed on family members.

At the centre of it all was the paramount place of the child most of all, and the family, and the community.

Children were considered supernatural gifts. Among other things, the Potlatch and its practices through ritual and ceremony taught us to honour universal laws of Namwayut.

————

AS WE INDIGENOUS begin to reconcile internally, we need to return to Genesis. We're hearing more and more from our leaders and Knowledge Keepers that before we get to know where we are going, we need to know where we come from. The most important lessons are those we find in our oral histories. Part of the reason for that is that we have to have faith and trust in our Elders, and in their lifelong volume of their learning.

Having these discussions about who we are with everybody—among cultures, among traditions, among families and individuals—would really make a big difference about understanding and mutual respect, and compassion for others while seeing that there are very few differences in our core values.

On our journey to reconciliation, without returning to our own beginning there will be little or no reconciliation. If you don't know who you are, how can you know where you come from and where you are going? For Indigenous families, a return to supernatural beginnings leads us to sacred sites.

Everything flows from that first spiritual manifestation. Our laws have been created through this millennial life force. Our ways of governance have risen through this process. Our economies have sustained us forever. Our political approach has protected us and foretells our future. Our culture has been shaped by the influence of our ancient tradition.

We sing, dance, laugh, and honour our interconnectedness. Absolutely everything about who we are as Indigenous Peoples can be tracked to our first ancestors.

So let us reflect for a moment on where we are as Indigenous Peoples by looking back, and then looking forward, to our foremost ancestral beginnings. And it provides us with hope; our Creation stories place us in spaces of belonging and connection. Our Genesis shaped and forged through all time.

That is, until the newcomers came.

———

CANADA HAS been charged with having committed genocide against Indigenous Peoples, and that is a part of this country's origin. This bombshell allegation was made in a summary report by Canada's Truth and Reconciliation Commission in June of 2015. The report said, in part, that for over a century the central goals of Canada's policies were to eliminate Indigenous governments, ignore Indigenous rights, terminate the treaties, and, through a process of assimilation, cause Indigenous Peoples to *cease to exist* as distinct legal, social, cultural, religious, and racial entities. The report stated that Indigenous Peoples experienced physical and cultural genocide—the destruction of those structures and practices that allowed us to thrive in the past. The establishment and operation of residential schools were a central element of this policy, which can best be described as cultural genocide.

Canada did all these things.

The reason that this collective knowledge is so important is that, at present, we are almost living simulated lives, lives that are so different from our natural state. This is just as true for all Canadians as it is for Indigenous Peoples and communities. There is something about Canada that is good, but at the same time, there is a part of me that feels that any good that any of us possessed at a time before assimilation has waned.

We have buckled from the impacts of colonialism, assimilation, and racism—all of us. Every one. And I think that's where racism continues to flourish, because we're forgiving, and we want everybody to simply be assimilated into a common understanding of the world. But when we become assimilated, usually we become less than the person we were before. Genocide represents the era that started when the newcomers arrived, who at first wanted to make us in their own image. Their collective attempts to achieve that aim were *so intentional* that it was eventually tagged by the Truth and Reconciliation Commission as genocide.

Can this be a moment of reckoning for all of us, we Canadians and Indigenous Peoples, in which we can reconcile?

We have a choice to make. In our Genesis, we started with a time of hope, promise, and positive evolution. Now we are in this moment where reconciliation awaits us. We can restore this evolution through mutual respect and understanding.

Indigenous Peoples have endured genocide. We've survived the constellation of colonization, assimilation, racism, and hatred. All our cultures and languages have been trampled upon. Our identities have been trashed through all of this. And yet, with our strength, resilience, and courage we still hold on to hope—hope that we will restore our common humanity. My Indigenous brothers and sisters, all my relatives, we have much to do internally as individuals to reconcile with ourselves. We have much to do as collectives to reconcile within our own connected communities. Trauma still impedes our own progress and development. We need to do that work as well as the work of societal reconciliation with others. We must return to the land and culture. We must re-enact and reclaim our ancestral values and teachings.

————

THE ANTIDOTE to genocide is the return to Genesis. That's what decolonization means.

Genesis.

Genocide.

Reconciliation.

———

BUT GENESIS is also important to all Canadians. Genesis is a starting point for change. We all have Genesis stories in our communities, our cultures, our families. Many of us have experienced genocide and a shared intergenerational trauma in Canada, Indigenous or not. Many of us experience racism, Indigenous or not. Arguing over competing narratives is not what is important. What is important to remember is that we all have our stories to tell.

There's one Creation, one humanity. We are all interconnected, one human world. One celestial space, one animal world, one undersea world, and a spirit world all needing balance and harmony. We believe in the importance of children.

Genesis, whether it starts with an origin on a mountaintop, or in a flood, or with Adam and Eve—it's about us. It is about people who, in their earliest consciousness, belonged to some level of purity that, for all of us, has continued to be eroded and diminished.

But every once in a while, humanity has a chance to realign with the universe. We're starting to feel again, those feelings of deep yearning that we don't even understand all the time. Feelings that there was something wonderful, at some point in the past, and that was the beginning.

Now we've come to our point of challenge, a collective higher level of difficulty. Confusion has disconnected us from who we are, and now, Genesis feels like a comfortable place to try to connect with again.

And maybe that's what is missing. Genesis is our missing spiritual place, that deep yearning and longing for *ourselves* that we've been so far removed from for a long time. Life has changed, and our perceptions and our truths have shifted, but we still sometimes stop and think: "My God, our Genesis can be our moment." We want to reach back and pull it toward us, that place, that point of origin, that oneness with our very essence. We want to bring it up to the moon, shine light on what we might be if we could just find it once more.

And sometimes, over the course of our lifetimes, when we reach one of those moments, they are ways for us to escape, just briefly, the hardship and trauma of our current reality.

When we experience racism, or disconnection, or we lose our sense of our own story, life can become a really lonely place. For newcomers now, when they are asked to assimilate into Canada in even the most benign of ways, it can heighten their sense of not belonging to this new place in which they now find themselves. And so, thinking about Genesis, thinking about who we are, becomes an important internal exercise, even if it's momentary.

Thinking about our origins can help us regain maybe just a slight degree of our humanity.

Our worth.

Our value.

Our integrity.

Integrity is our last line of defence against hatred, fear, racism, and all that is causing us pain.

Finding our home, living in our own skin, embracing who we are, and honouring our authentic selves are all a critical part of this, so it doesn't matter how much prejudice or wrongful assumptions come your way.

You know who you are.

Your values and principles are right there with you.

You have a sense of dignity and belonging that will never fade.

My speech at the University of British Columbia's
Convocation (2003). *Photo: Martin Dee*

Left: A view of the Walk for Reconciliation. *Photo: Hamid Attie*

Below: Speaking at the 2013 Walk for Reconciliation, our first. *Photo: Hamid Attie*

Above: My grandson Thunder and me.

Right: My granddaughter Stephanie, me, and my daughter Shelley.

Facing top: My son Bob Joseph and my grandson Rodman.

Facing bottom: Billy Robertson, me, William Wasden, and Robert Chamberlain, with my grandson Thunder behind us.

Above: My daughter Karen, who arranged the first Walk for Reconciliation, me, and my grandchildren Sadie and Thunder. *Photo: Hamid Attie*

Facing top: My dear son Farrell and me at the Walk for Reconciliation.

Facing bottom: The great artist Chief Beau Dick and me.

Just me.

(19)

THE COVENANT

RECONCILIATION HAS given me a gift.

It is you who give me hope. It is you who give me inspiration. You are here, sharing these stories with me, witnessing me, and, I hope, opening yourself up to be witnessed. That's all I know, right now. As we move forward, day after day, engaging with each other, we learn more about each other. Already, some responses to our human condition have started to come forward, in what you feel in reading these words.

And that's all it takes.

All it takes is a moment to embrace something, something that has a chance to morph, to grow. To become critical mass. Nobody knew how many people would show up to care about reconciliation, or about each other, or Indigenous Peoples, or Canadians. And the beauty of all that, when you think about it and look back, is that on the other side of the darkness, we're coming to a point of discovery of our potential as human beings.

We began to see a fuller picture of humanity, not just Indigenous Peoples. Not just Canadians. And it has to be that way. Because we all live here in one place that we share together. I don't know if we could ever achieve reconciliation if we didn't hold the view that reconciliation means something for all of us—that we're all beneficiaries, that we're all contributors. And then at the end, we act in good faith toward each other.

As we move away from the darker periods of our history, we must do so with a certainty of conviction that older prevailing attitudes of superiority and inferiority are not a part of the equation. Our sense of collective well-being must be maintained and guarded to protect the integrity of our whole society. Meanwhile, as we contemplate additional newcomers, we must also build the cornerstones to a strong and viable society to which we invite these peoples. Let us have a deeper dialogue about this issue. Let us develop meaningful relationships that honour our past and our present. Let us as citizens in our own communities take responsibility for welcoming our newcomers. Let us encourage our children to walk together where they live. Let us celebrate our differences in diversity into a collective that gives untold richness of fabric and spirit.

We are all responsible for this future.

Namwayut is a powerful word that calls us to our highest self in just a small moment of quiet, and in our big, noisy, boisterous, significant moments. Even so, every time that word is conjured up, we are reminded that we are one *in* this universe, and we are one *with* the universe.

Namwayut is a core value.

Namwayut is a kind of magic.

Namwayut is who we are.

When I started to see myself as part of a whole, when I reconciled with myself, everything changed for me. I suddenly realized that my well-being depended on my connecting with others, sharing others' stories, understanding others' gifts.

I learned that, in terms of pure love and happiness, I had to be open to all people. I learned that whether you have business with them or not, give others a salutary greeting, a nod. Be respectful, as people know when you're respectful. And slowly, doing so allows you to have the sense of integrating back into the whole. I remember clearly my time of shame, embarrassment, humiliation, and the pain of being close to death, both physical and emotional. As I reconciled with myself, I became aware of new things happening for me.

People loved me, because I was loving.

People loved me, because I laughed at myself and laughed with them.

People loved me, because they knew I wasn't looking down on them or making judgments.

People loved me because they recognized that whatever my role was, it was to enhance everyone, including myself.

In acknowledging this need for openness, I suddenly was transformed from a person who did not know love to one who felt only love. Knowing this became my gift, and this allowed me to integrate my purpose, to be aligned with why I was put on this Earth. When and where I work, I reach out so that I may impact others through my acts of love.

Love is the place where Granny came from. Love is where Tom Dawson came from. And love is where I come from now.

———

RECONCILIATION CAN be a spiritual covenant. Reconciliation has to have an element of spiritual cooperation and commitment so that it's binding, and so that it invokes the best in all of us. We all belong here. And so let this be our covenant.

Let us call in our highest selves, our human consciousness, in wanting something bigger, better for all of us.

Let us remember that in spite of what we have done to ourselves, we belong and we are loved.

Let us always know that love is the foundation of everything: for the universe, for the world around us, for family, for self.

Let us call in our spirit of witness, and hear each other's stories of pain, of joy, and of hope.

Let us take on a responsibility to each other, and let our every action be in the highest interest of the collective.

Let us create the magic of the universe for our children, and welcome each child into the fold with constant and abiding love.

Let us align people together, even if it's for a second, or a moment, or an hour, or a day, and connect our energies, our hearts and minds, our souls.

Let us—every faith, every colour, every creed—recognize our common humanity.

Let us accept the truth that we are all one.

EPILOGUE
APOLOGIES MATTER

HE RECENT papal apology by Pope Francis in March 2022 matters.

It matters because Survivors have been calling for apologies for a long time, including one from the Vatican.

It matters because the Truth and Reconciliation Commission of Canada, in its Calls to Action 58–61, calls for an apology from the Pope.

It matters because Survivors need formal acknowledgement of their pain, suffering, and loss.

It matters because Survivors demand accountability from those responsible for inflicting the harm and trauma imposed upon them.

It matters because apologies can serve to peel away the walls of denial and expose the full truth.

It matters to Survivors because apologies can serve as stepping stones to continued healing and reconciliation in their lives.

It matters so that the world can learn more about the tyranny of colonization and the spectre of genocide in places like Canada.

The federal government, RCMP, and the mainstream churches involved in the operation of residential schools have all apologized. While the independent Roman Catholic entities in Canada apologized, this proved insufficient for Survivors who favoured an apology directly from the Pope who represents the full body of the Roman Catholic Church. Two delegations to Rome later, including a group in 2008 led by former National Chief Phil Fontaine and the most recent trip in late March 2022, we have an apology.

That's how it works, how miracles unfold. Brick by brick, step by step.

Pope Francis has promised to come to Canada shortly, and we can build on the apology that was made.

The brilliance of the Truth and Reconciliation Commission report and its commissioners, Justice Murray Sinclair, Chief Willie Littlechild, and Marie Wilson must be heeded *and honoured*, especially at this time with respect to Calls to Action 58–61.

And I have one final thought. Apologies are not etched in stone, but they can serve as fertile ground to be catalysts for change and transformation.

Let us support and advocate for a fulsome papal apology by Pope Francis when he comes to Canada later this year.

Let us always remember the approximately 150,000 Indigenous children who languished in the over 130 residential schools that operated. Top of mind at the moment are the growing numbers of unmarked graves found on former residential school sites. Know that over 4,100 deaths at residential schools have been documented and that this may only be the tip of the iceberg.

We must prepare ourselves as Indigenous Peoples to be involved and engaged in the heavy work of healing and reconciliation. It has begun with us and our own families and communities as it should, especially among those of us still here who have weathered the incalculable harm and trauma in the wake of residential schools. For many of us, we will be struggling to overcome the harm, but we must for the sake of our children and generations to come.

Let us use all the tools that exist to foster continued healing and reconciliation:

- Canada's Truth and Reconciliation Commission report and its 94 Calls to Action

- The United Nations Declaration on the Rights of Indigenous Peoples (UNDRIP)

- The Missing and Murdered Indigenous Women and Girls report's 231 Calls for Justice

- Breathing life into the residential school apologies by turning words into actions.

- The currently unfathomable will by Canadians to engage in reconciliation, which is remarkable.

- The existing degree and volume of efforts made across the spectrum of society, and the degree and volume of reconciliation efforts and initiatives already underway in Canada, the level of which, you may discover, is surprising.

We must stay the course.

GLOSSARY

Ada (ah-dah) mother (used for grandmother today)
A̱m'lilas (uhm-lee-lahs) playroom
A̱nisbidu' (ah-nees-bee-do) little aunty
Atła̱k'ima (ah-tlah-gee-mah) forest-spirit kingdom

Ba̱k'wa̱s (buh-gwuhs) wild man of the woods
Baxwbakwalanuksiwe' (bahwx-bah-kwalah-nook-see-wey)
    man-eater spirit from the North End of the World

Dła̱xwe' (dlah-xweh) social standing
Duxw'wida's (doox-wee-dahs) you look
Dzunuk'wa (dzoo-noo-gwah) forest giants—wild woman
    of the woods

G̱ilakas'la, Długwe' (gee-lah-kas-lah dloo-gweh) greetings,
    my supernatural one
G̱ilakas'la, Wołkine' (gee-lah-kas-lah wolh-kineh)
    greetings, my supernatural gift
G̱ilga'lis (gill-gah-lees) first one here

233

Gilsgamlił (gills-gum-leelh) first to appear curtain
  ceremony

Gukwdzi (gukwh-dzee) Big House (ceremonial)

Gwa'yasdam's (gwa-yahs-dums) feasting place—Gilford
  Island

Gwa'yi (gwah-yee) Kingcome village, Kingcome River

Gwa'yimdzi (gwah-yihm-dzee) big whale

Hinumagame' (hee-new-gah-meh) lead hereditary Chief

K'u'łustola (goo-lhoos-toe-lah) the bubbling wellspring

Kwinxwala'ogwa (quin-xwa-lah-oh-gwah)
  Thunderbird lady

Laxu'k'wala (lah-xoo-gwa-lah) coughing sickness,
  i.e., tuberculosis

ł'na (dlee-nah) eulachon oil

'Mim'kwamlis (mihm-kwum-lees) islands in front—
  Village Island

Na'di (nah-dee) little girl (term of endearment)

'Namgis (num-gees) Nimpkish River Tribe

'Namima (nah-mee-mah) people of one kind—clan

Namwayut (num-wee-yut) those with whom you are one

Nawalakw (na-wah-laqw) the supernatural, the sacred

Nogad (noh-gahd) one who carries wisdom

'Nula'yi (noo-lah-yee) eldest one

Nuyimagiwe' (new-yih-mah-gee-wey) lead ancestor
  (lead story)

Nuyimbalis (new-yihm-bah-lees) a story throughout
   time and forever

P'asa (buh-sah) Potlatching business

Sibalxola (see-bull-xhoh-lah) sound of copper ringing

Sisiyuł (see-see-yulh) supernatural double-headed
   serpent

Ugwanu (oo-gwah-noo) white-haired on the sides

'Walas Gwa'yim (wah-lus gwa-yihm) Chief Beau Dick,
   great whale

'Walas ikin noka'yes kas yuwakus lox I am so happy that
   you are here

Waxawidi (wah-xha-wee-dee) Chief William Wasden,
   canoes come to his shore

Yalis (yah-lees) spread-leg beach

Yax'id (yah-xheed) to die

Yo, 'Wadzid (yoh wah-dzeed) hello, monumental one

ACKNOWLEDGEMENTS

ACKNOWLEDGE my family for their unwavering support in the writing of this book, which gave rise to our discovery of common good, hope, and purpose: my wife, Donna; my three sons, Bob Jr, Frank, and Farrell; and my two daughters, Karen and Shelley.

I also acknowledge Page Two for their remarkable array of professional experts who left no stone unturned to provide me with the best advice and editorial guidance. Special thanks to Rony Ganon, project manager, for her inspirational and dedicated support. Kudos to the gentle and caring support from Amanda Lewis, my editor. Thank you to marketing manager Chris Brandt for your generosity and kindness. This book could not have been completed without the collective support from Page Two team members including co-founder Trena White, copy editor Lisa Frenette, creative director Peter Cocking, and photographer Hamid Attie. Thank you, Page Two, Raincoast, and Macmillan.

A very special nod to my writing collaborator, Lisa Thomas-Tench, who breathed added spirit into this narrative.

I humbly bow to the brilliant and talented young Kwakwaka'wakw artist Nagedzi, Andy Everson, who, for the case of this book, created and captured my vision of the universe!

Thank you, Royal BC Museum, for the use of your pictures.

I acknowledge the countless hands and organizations that have forged a path forward for us to consider as we advance continued healing, reconciliation, and justice. These organizations include the National Indian Residential School Survivors Society, BC Indian Residential School Survivors Society, Aboriginal Healing Foundation, Legacy of Hope Foundation, Reconciliation Canada, Truth and Reconciliation Commission of Canada (TRC), TRC Elders Council, Shingwauk Alumni Society (Ontario), Shubenacadie Residential School (Nova Scotia), Spirit Wind (Manitoba), Voluntary Roundtable for Truth and Reconciliation as called for by the Royal Commission on Aboriginal Peoples and Georges Erasmus and invited by the United Church, Settlement Agreement (SA) Parties, Independent Assessment Process Secretariat, Vancouver All Faith Roundtable, and Reconciliation Canada Elder Advisers.

I acknowledge some of the champions who blazed the way for us in our search for truth, justice, healing, and reconciliation including Mario Dion, ADM of Indian Residential Schools Resolution Canada; the Honourable Justice Frank Iacobucci, SA Negotiator; former National Chief Phil Fontaine; Mike DeGagné, Aboriginal Healing Foundation; David MacDonald, Anglican Church representative, Settlement Agreement Party; Jamie Scott, United Church representative to SA; Mike Cachagee, National Indian Residential School Society; Ted Quewezance, National Indian Residential School Society; Sharon Thira, BC Indian Residential School Survivors Society; Steven Point, former Lieutenant Governor of British Columbia; Maggie Hodgson, Leader in Aboriginal health, justice, and reconciliation; Alvin Dixon, IRSSS frontline advocate; Yvonne Rigsby-Jones, former Executive Director, Tsow-Tun Le Lum Society; Ed John, First Nations Summit; Stewart Phillips, Union of BC Indian Chiefs; Jody Wilson-Raybould, BC Assembly of First Nations.

I acknowledge the following people as well: Charlene Belleau, Ray Mason, Grace Eiko Thomson, Robbie Waisman, Farid Rohani, Dan Rubenstein and Nancy Dyson, and Dr Lillian Howard. In addition, I thank Willie Blackwater and the Willie Blackwater Plaintiffs Group. Thank you in memoriam to Ted Hughes and Candy Palmater. Kudos to Glenn Sigurdson, Shane Pointe, Arlene Roberts, and Gerry Oldman, and all the Indian Residential School Survivors Society Board of Directors and staff. I am grateful to Bob Watts, Peter Grant, and David Paterson. Thank you for your work

Cindy Blackstock, Mary Ellen Turpel-Lafond, Kathleen Mahoney, and Paulette Regan. I acknowledge the support of Rudy and Caroline North, Don Lindsay, Linda Norris, Tamara Vrooman, Kevin McCort, and Arlene Strom. Thank you to Barney Williams and your TRC Elders committee members. Much obliged, Stephen Kafki. I acknowledge Madeleine MacIvor, Linc Kesler, and Dr Jo-ann Archibald.

Finally, thank you to my family, Pauline Alfred, Stan Hunt, Stan Wamiss, and my dear friend John McCandless.

Chiefs William Wasden and Beau Dick, I thank you.

BIBLIOGRAPHY

Galois, Robert. *Kwakwaka'wakw Settlements,*
1775–1920: A Geographical Analysis and Gazetteer.
UBC Press, 1994.

Harper, Stephen. "Statement of Apology to
Former Students of Indian Residential Schools."
Government of Canada, 2008.

Truth and Reconciliation Commission of Canada.
The Final Report of the Truth and Reconciliation Com-
mission of Canada: Honouring the Truth, Reconciling
for the Future. Vol. 1. James Lorimer, 2015.

ABOUT THE AUTHOR

CHIEF DR ROBERT JOSEPH, OBC, OC is a true peacebuilder whose life and work are examples of his personal commitment. A Hereditary Chief of the Gwawaenuk First Nation, Chief Joseph has dedicated his life to bridging the differences brought about by intolerance, lack of understanding, and racism at home and abroad.

His insights into the destructive impacts these forces can have on peoples' lives, families, and cultures were shaped by his experience within Canada's Indian residential school system. As one of the last few speakers of the Kwak'wala language, Chief Joseph is an eloquent and inspiring ceremonial house speaker. He shares his knowledge and wisdom in the Big House, as a language speaker with the University of British Columbia, as an internationally recognized art curator, and as coauthor of *Down from the Shimmering Sky: Masks of the Northwest Coast.*

In 2003, Chief Joseph received an Honorary Doctorate of Law degree from the University of British Columbia for his distinguished achievements in serving British Columbia and Canada. In 2012, he was presented the Diamond Jubilee Medal by the Right Honourable David Johnston, Governor General of Canada. In 2014, he received the Jack P. Blaney Award for Dialogue from Simon Fraser University and an Honorary Doctorate of Divinity from Vancouver School of Theology for his work on reconciliation and renewing relationships between Indigenous Peoples and all Canadians. That same year, the City of Vancouver awarded Chief Joseph with the Diversity and Inclusion Award of Excellence. In 2015, he was presented a Deputy Minister's Recognition Award for Collaboration and Partnerships and was appointed to the Order of British Columbia, the province's highest honour. Chief Joseph was also named as one of the "50 Most Powerful People in Vancouver" by *Vancouver Magazine*. In 2016, he received the Wallenberg-Sugihara Civil Courage Award and the Indspire Lifetime Achievement Award. In 2017, Chief Joseph was named an officer of the Order of Canada for his dedication to the community and contributions to the country. In 2018, he received an Honorary Doctorate of Law from Vancouver Island University.

Chief Joseph is currently the Ambassador for Reconciliation Canada and a member of the National

Assembly of First Nations Elders Council. He was formerly the Executive Director of the Indian Residential School Survivors Society and is an honorary witness to Canada's Truth and Reconciliation Commission. As Chairman of the Native American Leadership Alliance for Peace and Reconciliation and Ambassador for Peace and Reconciliation with the International Interreligious Federation for World Peace, Chief Joseph has sat with the leaders of South Africa, Israel, Japan, South Korea, Mongolia, and the United States to learn from and share his understanding of faith, hope, healing, and reconciliation.

namwayut.com